understanding the
Planetary Myths

understanding the
Planetary Myths

lisa tenzin-dolma

quantum
LONDON • NEW YORK • TORONTO • SYDNEY

quantum

An imprint of W. Foulsham & Co. Ltd
The Publishing House, Bennetts Close, Cippenham, Slough,
Berkshire, SL1 5AP, England

ISBN 0-572-03032-0

Cover illustration by Jurgen Ziewe

A CIP record for this book is available from the British Library

Printed in Great Britain by Creative Print and Design (Wales), Ebbw Vale

Contents

Preface		7
About the Author		8
Acknowledgements		9
Introduction		11
The Planets		19
CHAPTER 1	In the Beginning ...	21
CHAPTER 2	The Sun – Apollo	25
CHAPTER 3	The Moon – Artemis / Diana	36
CHAPTER 4	Mercury – Hermes	44
CHAPTER 5	Venus – Aphrodite	53
CHAPTER 6	Mars – Ares	63
CHAPTER 7	Jupiter – Zeus	72
CHAPTER 8	Saturn – Cronus	82
CHAPTER 9	Uranus – Uranus	92
CHAPTER 10	Neptune – Poseidon	101
CHAPTER 11	Pluto – Hades	111

The Asteroids   123

CHAPTER 12	Chiron – Chiron	125
CHAPTER 13	Ceres – Demeter	134
CHAPTER 14	Juno – Hera	146
CHAPTER 15	Pallas Athene – Athena	158
CHAPTER 16	Vesta – Hestia	169
CHAPTER 17	Relationships and Aspects	178
CHAPTER 18	Harmonising the Voices	185
	Archetypal Rulerships	188
	Index	189

Preface

The planets and asteroids are named after Roman and Greek gods and goddesses whose stories have their roots in Ancient Greece. Through knowing the myths of these archetypal figures, it is possible to easily understand why each planet and asteroid has a particular interpretation in a horoscope. The relationships between these deities can also shed light on the interpretation of aspects made by planets to each other in the natal chart.

Myths and stories provide a subtle form of information that is easily and naturally assimilated. This book is intended as an informative, entertaining and interesting guide to the myths that underpin the principles of the planets, and explains why each has its own specific symbolism in the study of astrology. The book will also appeal to readers who are interested in the significance of myth in our lives.

In each chapter, the myth is told in story form. This is followed by an explanation of the symbolism of the archetype, and concludes with a description of the traditional qualities embodied by the corresponding planet or asteroid when interpreted in a natal chart reading.

About the Author

Lisa Tenzin-Dolma has been intrigued by stories and symbolism since childhood, and realised early on that the characters in the myths struck sympathetic chords with specific areas of the psyche that then reflected outwardly through life experiences. Her curiosity about the workings of the mind led her to the study of astrology in 1979, when her eldest son was born. Through this she discovered an interest in the powerful resonances between the planets and their myths, which she developed over the years. Her fascination with the external expression of various archetypes led her to explore these through many different areas of work: as a musician, nurse, astrologer, aromatherapist, counsellor, designer, cook, medical laboratory assistant, proofreader, artist and writer.

Lisa is the author and illustrator of *The Glastonbury Tarot* and the author of *The Dolphin Experience* and *Swimming with Dolphins* (W. Foulsham & Co. Ltd 0-572-02364-2). She lives in Bath, England.

For Lisa Blatchly

Acknowledgements

Writing a book is similar to giving birth to a child. There is the conception of the idea, the inner absorption as it takes shape within you, the transition between the mysterious beauty of the blank pages of possibility and the emergence of the child born of thought; the solid reality as it takes form in its entirety. Many people are involved during the gestation period, during the time before it is handed over to those who will clothe it and speed its way into the wider world.

Wendy Hobson, my editor at Foulsham, encouraged me to develop the ideas that led to the writing of this book. She and Christine Harris, who prepared the manuscript for publication, acted as midwives. Wendy's belief in the book, and Christine's dedication to easing its journey into the world, provided the opportunity for joyful birth.

For sustenance on all levels I have my family to thank: my parents and sister, for planting the seeds during my early years by showing me that each country we lived in was our home, for firing my curiosity, encouraging me with stories and leading me to the library in each new town; my children, for soaking up the tales of the myths before and after this book was conceived, asking questions that led me towards fresh views of the scenery of the mind and imagination, and never complaining about erratic mealtimes.

Friends provided emotional nourishment and stimulating discussion. Loving thanks are extended to the storytellers *par excellence* among them who continually inspire me to try harder: Annie Dalton, Joanne Harris, Lynne Benton, Poppy Palin, Crysse Morrison, Jill Smith and everyone in the writing groups. Added warmth and enthusiasm came from Marcus and Liz Blosch, Linda Watt, Catherine Norwood-Aird, Karen Linford, Harriet Oldridge,

John Yallup, Keith Phillips, Anthony Zappia, Sam and Stuart, and Carole Negre. At *MBS Magazine,* my editors, Jenni Cole, Emma Tennant, Sarah Burnside and Jane Burgess thoughtfully extended article deadlines to allow me the space to write this book.

And last but certainly not least, I acknowledge my debt to the poet Homer, whose *Odyssey* and *Iliad,* read and absorbed in my childhood, sparked the ideas that led me along the pathways of the mind and provided the foundation for my fascination with mythology; and Bruno and Louise Huber, who many years ago taught me the principles of astrological psychology.

Introduction

T he cosmos is a complex symphony of energy that, through all of its many forms of expression, is composed of individual notes. These notes come together to create chords in the form of galaxies and solar systems, which are in turn reflected in miniature within the cellular structures in our bodies and, smaller still, the quantum worlds. The word 'universe' means 'one song'. A study of the physical sciences, quantum physics and cosmology, as well as of metaphysics, shows us that everything in existence is subtly connected.

We know that the Moon exerts a powerful influence on the tides and, because our bodies are mostly composed of water, we feel the pull of the Moon's cycles within ourselves. Sunspot activity affects electrical systems on Earth and the electro-magnetic charges within our cells. We are all part of a universe that is expressed holographically, with the image of the whole contained within each of its parts. This means that each of us touches, and is touched by, the mystery of the worlds around us, within us and beyond our planet.

Astrology is the study of the influences of the constellations and planets on our lives. The 'musical note' of each planet resonates with the vibrational notes of our inner nature to create elements of harmony or discord within the psyche that affect our inner and outer self-expression. The relationships between one planet and another, and their placement in the heavens at the moment of your birth, have effects that are felt in varying degrees throughout your life. A knowledge of the mythological symbolism of the planets at the moment of your birth can help you to understand more about who you are and can enable you to interpret the complex combinations of signs and symbols, houses and aspects, in a more immediate, personal manner.

The study of astrology is intended to foster a sense of self-empowerment and self-understanding. Your natal chart gives indications of how you can develop your potential to its fullest. It shows character traits, attitudes, gifts and weaknesses. These can all be worked with. Gifts can be developed; challenges can be overcome and viewed as tools that help you to develop strength of character and compassion. We, in essence, are more than merely the sum of the planetary influences that prevailed at the time of birth – our innate potential is vast. Yet we can be greatly enriched through understanding those influences, by seeing how and why we act and react in certain ways. Unhealthy patterns can be discarded, new possibilities can be explored and our lives can become more fulfilling.

Archetypes and Myths

The planets and asteroids represent archetypal forces that we all contain within us. An archetype is an instinctual mental image, an imprint that resides deep within the collective unconscious and is common to all cultures. In modern times, the word 'archetype' is used to describe something that is the first of its kind; that sets off a new pattern and is used as a basis for further development. Our interpretation and recognition of a particular archetype is based upon our cultural and philosophical conditioning. The Great Mother would be embodied by Mary for Christians, by Gaia for the Ancient Greeks, by Isis for the Egyptians. Whatever your belief system, you will be instinctively attuned to a particular set of archetypes. In astrology, the planets and asteroids each hold an archetypal resonance, and the prominence or inconspicuousness of each of these can be viewed as the weft and warp in the colourful, complex tapestry of your personality.

A myth is an ancient, traditional, usually sacred story that concerns the spiritual journey of an archetypal figure. Every culture has a rich seeding of myths that underpin the history, beliefs and development of that culture. These myths are surprisingly similar; there is much common ground, however diverse the culture, no matter how distant the country of origin from our own.

Through myth, we are attuned to something that seems greater than ourselves. The stories that arise through an exploration of the mythic realms are tales of the adventures of larger-than-life characters: gods and beasts, heroes and demons. Myths take the listener on a journey through the inner self, where we can identify with, rejoice in, or be horrified by, the amplification of the many facets of human nature. Stories have long been used as a tool for educating as well as entertaining. You can become absorbed in a story, can travel through a mysterious realm into a place where myth and magic are real, where fantasies and fears can be played out safely. Stories can be a guide for life, giving us clues as to how to find our way through the often labyrinthine situations we find ourselves in. You can even view your own life as a myth, for our lives are rich in stories; we all experience tests, trials, struggles, joys, triumphs and celebrations. This quest that we undertake at birth, and continue through to the last breath, is played out against a backdrop of other characters who bring out the best and the worst in us, who challenge or reward us. Ultimately, we create our own mythic life from the materials around and within us.

The words 'myth' and 'mythic' are sometimes interpreted as implying a sense of unreality, of fabrication, of illusion. We weave myths and legends around the exploits of those who seem too distanced from us to be quite human. The mythical man or woman takes on a larger life, a greater role, than we can perhaps imagine experiencing ourselves, yet their exploits fire the imagination and encourage us to dream and to bring those dreams into reality. Myths act as a reminder of possibilities.

The Place of Myth

The cultures of the world developed with their reliance on myths as a constant reminder of the sacred mystery of life. Myths were also used as moral tales and as a connection between the puzzle of purpose in humanity and the sense of meaning derived from tales of the omnipresent, omniscient, omnipotent forces that watched over humankind and sometimes interceded or interfered in human affairs.

The old gods and goddesses are not dead to the psyche, and woe betide us should we attempt to bury them completely. The taboos and laws enforced since ancient times by mythological story, and the spiritual and temporal codes and laws that resulted, created a place for us in the universe. When we lose sense of that place, we lose an essential connection with our spiritual nature. This is reflected in society as increased confusion, violence, mental illness, and apathy, and an upsurge in the use of recreational drugs or prescribed chemicals that blast open the avenues of exploration without the foundation of wisdom and without guides or mentors. Myth gave rise to morals and to religion, even though the morals of the immortal deities appeared to be questionable at times.

Science and Myth

Science and myth, once considered to reside at opposite poles, are in truth two sides of the same coin. Myth provides a backdrop to science and helps us to find ways in which to explore and explain our inner as well as outer terrain.

Most world myths begin with Chaos — the Void. Within this maelstrom of uncontrollable, unpredictable energy, consciousness stirred and woke, bursting forth to birth the elements of the universe with all its diverse forms. Science, with its theories about the Big Bang, tells a story not too distanced from the myths in terms of sheer extraordinary, unimaginable power. The branch of physics devoted to chaos theory investigates how order emerges in unpredictable, inexplicable ways. Taken symbolically, the ideas are markedly similar.

The seven 'planets' (for astrological purposes) visible to the naked eye (the Sun, Moon, Mercury, Venus, Mars, Jupiter and Saturn) embody more than merely a symbolic astrological and astronomical resonance. They are embedded in our culture, bequeathing associations with the days of the week, the musical notes of our diatonic scale, and the original seven stems of learning – grammar, logic, rhetoric, arithmetic, music, geometry and astronomy. These subjects were initially understood through their associations with the planets, and nowhere is this now more relevant than in the study of the mind. Our mental states filter down to affect our emotional and physical health and well-being.

Freud surmised that 'a myth is a public dream; a dream is a private myth.' Jung took the view that myths are linked to the symbolic language of the psyche that helps us to recognise and integrate the inner wisdom of humankind that has always been there, locked within us. Myths are a key that opens a door into the deep self. The human spirit needs myth for sustenance, just as the human body needs fuel for energy and the human mind needs the understanding of the world and our place in it that the sciences give us.

The Planets and Mythology

The planets and asteroids that you interpret symbolically in your birth chart are named after Greek and Roman deities. The characteristics attributed to them are modelled on the qualities and traits of these pre-Christian gods and goddesses, whose stories in turn stem from the pantheon of Ancient Greece. Each deity has their own myth, and these myths intermingle because complex relationships exist between them. Together, they encompass all of the areas that we experience and explore within ourselves. Birth (the Sun), growth and change (the Moon), communication (Mercury), love (Venus), assertiveness (Mars), expansion (Jupiter), responsibility (Saturn), innovation (Uranus), mysticism (Neptune), and death (Pluto) are the realms of the planetary gods and goddesses. The myths of the asteroids, the chunks of rock that float through the asteroid belt between Mars and Jupiter, add extra depth. Healing (Chiron), nurturing (Ceres), conjoining (Juno), understanding (Pallas Athene) and compassion (Vesta) are the qualities that they embody. If you understand the story of each deity, and the subtleties of their relationships with each other, you can see how those energies work through the blueprint of your horoscope. Each planet and asteroid has a particular myth, a special influence, and this is played out in the arena of the signs and houses of the natal chart that each heavenly body is found in at the moment of birth.

If you view the planets and asteroids as aspects of yourself, you will be able to discover which ones you express most fluently, and which are repressed, denied or ignored. The crux of any system of self-understanding, astrology included, is the striving towards wholeness, the full integration and acceptance of yourself. Myth can be a useful and inspiring tool for this.

Greeks and Romans

Most of the planets and asteroids carry the names of Roman deities. However, the stories connected with these archetypes emerge from Ancient Greek myths, and these provide the foundation for the stories in this book. The Romans renamed some of the gods and reinterpreted their qualities and myths: one such was Eros, who metamorphosed from a primal creative force who escorted Aphrodite to Olympus after her emergence from the sea, into Cupid, with his bow and arrow. But the personalities of the deities whose names were given to the planets are largely unchanged. It is interesting to note that the outer planets, which were discovered comparatively recently, were allocated names from within the former pantheons. Uranus, though originally named Herschel, after the astronomer who discovered the planet, is known more commonly by the name of the Greek god, and the interpretations of these outer planets are closely linked with their namesakes.

The Sun god was Apollo, and the Moon goddess Artemis, whom the Romans called Diana. Hermes was renamed Mercury in the Roman pantheon. Aphrodite became known as Venus, and Ares as Mars. Zeus became Jupiter. Cronus was renamed Saturn. Uranus was given his Greek name. Poseidon became known as Neptune, and Hades as Pluto. With the asteroids, Chiron kept his Greek name, Demeter became known as Ceres, Hera as Juno, Athena as Pallas Athene, and Hestia became Vesta. In order to explore their stories in more depth, the section of each chapter that describes the mythological aspect uses the Greek name. The astrological resonances with the myths use the Roman name that we are more familiar with in astrology.

The Mythological Family

The ancient deities on which archetypal astrology is based can be viewed as musical notes in the symphony of the mind. Each of these notes is heard as a voice within the psyche that we 'tune in to' depending upon our focus. Some are loud and clear; others form background music. When combined through the aspects between the planets (the relationships of each planet to the others), some are harmonious, whereas others create discord. Each has its own voice and each will speak out at some point, even if that voice is quieter than the others. The positions of the planets and asteroids in your birth chart reveal which archetypal notes are loudest within you, and which whisper softly. Because all of these can be understood as aspects of ourselves, we can decide whether a voice can be coaxed into making itself heard more clearly. Or we can choose to quieten the one that dominates too frequently. We write the musical score of our lives through setting together the notes in the way that best suits our purposes.

Let us look at the notes in this symphony more closely. Once you listen to them individually, you can discover their places in your own psyche, and see how their vibrant notes add to the verses and choruses of your own psychological song.

The Planets

A round 4.6 billion years ago a nebula, a giant cloud of gas and dust, was drawn inwards by gravitational forces and began to collapse into itself. The combined force of gravity and increased density made the nebula spin faster and faster as it contracted, until it looked rather like a child's spinning top in the cosmic playground. The dense matter clumped together and birthed our sun, and the planets and asteroids, each held in place by the Sun's gravitational pull.

The planets took on their own defining qualities according to their distance from the Sun and their individual orbits. Like dewdrops in a sensitive web of vibrating strands, the Sun and planets each exerted their influence over the others from the beginning, exchanging resonances that affected the growth and development of all. Some effects were subtle, others more noticeable. Jupiter's gravitational pull, as its orbit moved closer to the Sun, caused sunspots that affected weather systems. The Moon acted on the tides on Earth. Debris from comets and asteroids that passed too close, or from the deaths of embryonic planets, left scars on planetary surfaces, and shifted orbits into different courses.

When humans appeared on Earth, they looked at the skies and saw patterns in the stars that each held stories and secrets. Curiosity led us to attempt to decipher those patterns; the symbols in the sky became a reflection of stories and symbols that emerged through the human psyche. And within the larger patterns of the constellations were stars that moved and could be tracked: the wanderers, the planets.

It became apparent that these wanderers also followed their own trails through the skies, and these paths, if observed carefully, could charter predictable courses. Some, like Mercury, moved swiftly. Others, the outer planets, moved slowly, taking years to cross an area of sky. And it was found that different configurations brought about particular influences. Astrology came into being.

Our need for story, the externalisation of the imagination, forged links between the myths that formed a cultural backdrop and the bright planets that made pinpoints in the canopy of night stars. The planets (and later the asteroids) were named after deities, and their astrological interpretations were based upon the personalities of these gods and goddesses. Even in modern times this still holds true. The ancients, through a blend of science, mysticism and intuition, observed connections that are forged as strongly as the gravitational forces that brought our solar system from a nebulous, gaseous state into a group of planets circling a star on an arm of the Milky Way galaxy.

In the Beginning...

The Olympian gods and goddesses whose stories are linked so powerfully to our solar system were not the first rulers in the mythology of Ancient Greece. The tale begins with Chaos, the state of flux from which all forms emerge. In modern times, as in the distant past, where memory, dreams and imagination created and destroyed worlds, Chaos lends its name to the maelstrom within which all possibilities reside. In the science of chaos theory, within that matrix of constantly shifting energy is found a plethora of what could be considered as miracles. The ancients were tuned in to this, and their myths reflect the contemporary perception of order arising out of disorder.

Floating on the sea of Chaos, the primeval state, was the Egg of Night. From this cosmic egg, symbol of the seed of creation, came Eros, the primal force, the embodiment of the principle of love. He used his arrows and torch to pierce through to the forms beneath, and illuminate them. Through Eros, a new world came into being.

Gaia, the Earth goddess, arose and provided a home for the deities of the future. She birthed Uranus, the sky god, who became her consort. Then came the mountains, nymphs and sea. The gods' realm encompassed the sky, earth and sea, night and day, darkness and light. The union of Gaia and Uranus brought forth the Titans Oceanus, Hyperion, Iapetus, Theia, Rhea, Themis, Mnemosyne, Phoebe, Tethys and Cronus.

But the survival of these primal deities appeared at first to be uncertain. Uranus, fearful that a child of his would take his power, imprisoned each newborn within Gaia's body to prevent their emergence from the earth. Eventually Gaia, understandably unhappy about the situation, devised a plan. When Cronus was born, she hid him in her depths and gave him a sickle made of sharp stone. The infant lay in wait, and when Uranus came to mate with Gaia, Cronus leaped out, severed the genitals of his father and threw them into the sea. The foam that rose from this birthed Aphrodite, the goddess of love and beauty. Stray drops of blood became the Erinyes (the Furies). Cronus released his siblings from the prison of their mother's body, and the Titans took power.

Cronus married Rhea and their union brought about Hestia, Demeter, Hera, Hades, Poseidon and Zeus. Fearful that he would lose his power to his children, Cronus swallowed each as it was born. Rhea, in desperation, turned to her parents for help during her pregnancy with Zeus. Gaia and Uranus told her to go to Crete, so she fled there to give birth, hid the infant in a cave, and gave Cronus a boulder wrapped in swaddling clothes, which he swallowed, thinking it was Zeus. Cared for secretly by his mother, Zeus grew strong and overthrew his father, then forced him to regurgitate his siblings. The stone that Cronus had mistaken for Zeus was placed at Delphi, the womb of the Earth. The new generation of gods, the Olympians, then took centre stage.

Ancient Greece

The topography of the Ancient Greeks was based on their belief that the world was flat and circular, and that their country was set in the centre of this disc, overshadowed by Mount Olympus, the home of

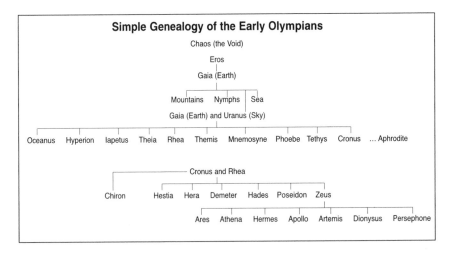

Simple Genealogy of the Early Olympians

Chaos (the Void)
|
Eros
|
Gaia (Earth)
|
Mountains   Nymphs   Sea
|
Gaia (Earth) and Uranus (Sky)

Oceanus   Hyperion   Iapetus   Theia   Rhea   Themis   Mnemosyne   Phoebe   Tethys   Cronus   ... Aphrodite

Cronus and Rhea

Chiron   Hestia   Hera   Demeter   Hades   Poseidon   Zeus

Ares   Athena   Hermes   Apollo   Artemis   Dionysus   Persephone

the gods who held power over the affairs of humankind. The Earth's disc was divided into two by the Mediterranean, which the Greeks called 'The Sea'. Surrounding the Earth was the 'River Ocean', which fed the central Sea.

The flat, circular Earth was subdivided according to the four directions. In the north dwelt the Hyperboreans. This land was inaccessible, and its inhabitants were said to live in a state of bliss, untrammelled by old age, disease or war. Later, Apollo, the Sun god, would travel there each year for sanctuary.

In the east was the realm of the dawn, and the Sun, Moon and stars. These rose from the eastern aspect of the Ocean, which surrounded the Earth, to travel across the sky, bringing light to the lives of both gods and mortals.

The south was inhabited by the Aethiopians, who lived in a similar state of peace and harmony to the Hyperboreans. These people were so favoured by the Olympians that the gods and goddesses would visit them and share in their feasts.

To the west lay the Elysian Plain, which was also called the 'Fortunate Fields' and the 'Isles of the Blessed'. This was the place where mortals favoured by the gods were taken to receive the gift of immortality.

Mount Olympus overlooked the Earth. Near its peak was a gateway of clouds that were guarded by the Seasons, who allowed safe passage to the gods and goddesses who had their home there.

When Cronus (Saturn) overthrew his father and ended the rule of the Titans, he married Rhea and fathered the new generation of Olympians. Their children were Zeus (Jupiter), Demeter (Ceres), Hera (Juno), Hades (Pluto), Poseidon (Neptune) and Hestia (Vesta). Later, Zeus fathered the next generation of Olympians, and the die was cast for myths that have endured over millennia.

Among these celestial beings were many others whose relevance is still felt. These included the nine Muses, who inspired poetry and song; the three Graces, who presided over all celebrations; the three Fates, who spun the threads of human destiny and cut these threads at the end of life; and the three Furies, who wreaked vengeance when justice was not done.

Each of the deities had a role to play, both in celestial and mortal affairs. Their mythical lives still inhabit the deep realms of the human mind. To the Ancient Greeks, they ruled from above and below — from the heavens, Earth, sea and underworld. In modern times their voices speak to us from within, sparked by our personal astrological connections and configurations and by our resonance with the aspects of our personalities that we most strongly relate to. The old gods are far from forgotten. Their influence still touches us and we can learn much from them.

CHAPTER TWO

The Sun
Apollo

The archetype of the Sun god is expressed through the essential symbolism of Apollo as the favourite son of Zeus / Jupiter, the ruler of the Olympians. As the one chosen to be the embodiment of leadership qualities, the son upon whom is pinned the mantle of succession to the throne, Apollo was trained from an early age to assume power and to view this as his birthright.

As the central focus of the solar system, the creative and generative force with its equal power to give and take life, the Sun holds a unique position. Apollo reflects this through his archetypal resonance. Like the Sun, he stands alone, set apart from his clan by the role bequeathed upon him by his father. His extrovert qualities are enhanced through his retreat to Hyperborea, a place where none can follow him. His nature is to shine his light on all, while holding silently to the mystery of his inner self.

The Birth of Apollo

Apollo was born on Delos, a barren Greek island, after a difficult nine-day labour. His mother, Leto, was a Titan, one of the forerunners of the Olympian gods, and she conceived Apollo and his twin sister, Artemis, when she was seduced by Zeus, the ruler of the Olympians. Zeus was notorious for his affairs, even though the jealousy of his long-suffering wife, Hera, was legendary and frequently accompanied by vengeful acts of retribution towards her husband's lovers. When Hera heard of the affair, she made it clear that anyone who helped Leto would be punished. So, alone and afraid, Leto wandered the Earth looking for a sanctuary where she could bring her children into the world. Eventually, in the final stages of labour, she arrived at the island that would later be named Delos, and gave birth to Artemis, goddess of the Moon, the hunt and childbirth.

Artemis helped with the arduous delivery of her brother, and Apollo was eventually born beneath a palm tree on the seventh day of the month. As he was being born, swans circled the island seven times, giving voice in celebration.

Exhausted from the trials she had endured, Leto handed Apollo over into the safekeeping of Themis, another pre-Olympian goddess, who nurtured him and raised him on nectar and ambrosia, the food of the gods. Her rulership of the art of prophecy was passed on to Apollo and she groomed him for a leadership role within the Olympian pantheon. His golden beauty, keen intellect and confident masculinity endeared him to Zeus, who gave him a chariot pulled by swans and appointed him as his favourite son. This chariot was used by Apollo to draw him on his daily journey across the sky and was also the vehicle that would take him in the future to the mystical realm of the Hyperboreans, a place in the north of Ancient Greece associated with the Pleiades constellation.

Personality Traits

Apollo was intensely inquisitive, with a tremendous thirst for knowledge. His keen intellect and abundant self-confidence made him the centre of attention, particularly where his father was concerned, which coincided with his planetary position as the brightest light in the sky. He was cheerful though somewhat detached and aloof, and sunny-natured, with the conviction that logic ruled supreme over emotion.

Yet Apollo was also extremely competitive. To come first, always to be the best, was the driving force behind his impulses and achievements. His methods were not always laudable, though to his mind they always seemed fair. To Apollo, logic was all-important. He was a thinker who refused to allow his emotions to take precedence. Although revered and respected for his mental clarity, his skill in archery and his power over the making and upholding of law and order, he needed time away from Olympia. He spent a year in retreat in Hyperborea and afterwards went there for three months each winter to replenish himself and allow the connection with his spiritual nature to be strengthened. This time marks the days on Earth when the Sun loses its warmth and fails to nurture the land.

His ability to aim for a goal and never miss his mark reflects the unerring confidence of those who are ruled astrologically by the Sun. The awareness of the goal creates an awareness of the future – of what can be sought and attained – and this ties in with Apollo's rulership of prophecy. He had a deep-rooted need to win, to be first in everything, and this driving force was backed up by a calculating quality that viewed the means as necessary to the end result. It was determination rather than emotion that drove him to attain his goals, and his ability for careful planning gave him a long-range view. Apollo embodies a striving for success and recognition.

Prophecy

The oracle at Delphi was situated at the base of Mount Parnassus. Delphi was considered to be the womb of the world, and its inner chamber was called the omphalos, which means 'navel'. The stone that Rhea gave to Cronus to swallow in place of Zeus was placed here. Beneath this mysterious space in the womb of the Earth, where clefts opened from deep within and gases mingled with the herbs burned to aid the oracle to access altered states of awareness, lived the Python, a great snake born from Gaia. The Python whispered to Pythia, the oracular priestess, who then intoned the information she had received. This was a female realm, embodying the intuition, the mystery of the unknown and the emergence of the knowledge of the deep self into the light of consciousness. Apollo's logic could not understand this and did not wish to. He sought control over the mystery and placed his own version of prophecy in its stead.

One of the first acts of Apollo was to take his golden bow and arrow and slay the Python. He put priestesses of his own in charge, who became known as Pythonesses, and their prophecies were interpreted by Apollo's priests, which ensured that control of this previously female domain was handed over to men. Gaia was outraged at the murder of her child and went to Zeus calling for retribution. To appease Gaia, Zeus insisted that Apollo become a slave to a mortal man for a period of time.

Apollo himself had no prophetic abilities, though the rulership of the oracle belonged to him and he could transfer the gifts of prophecy to others. People came to the oracle for help and advice and for purification. From this place, Apollo dispensed justice and made laws.

The innermost chamber at Delphi contained the grave of Dionysus, the god of wine and ecstasy. During the three months of each year when Apollo retreated to Hyperborea, Dionysus had charge of the temple. These half-siblings, both with Zeus as their father, were diametrically opposite in temperament. The nature of Dionysus was abandoned and wild, given to excess in drinking, dancing and lovemaking. The contrast between Apollo's government of the oracle and that of Dionysus indicates that, even when all efforts are made to suppress the wild self, it must re-emerge when the civilised self temporarily steps back.

Relationships

Apollo was not always lucky in love. His lovers were chosen for their beauty, intelligence and independence, but he often chose women who were his opposite in nature and was rejected by them; the cool, logical impulses craved union with the fey, sensitive, psychic aspect of femininity that his detached rational mind could not understand. Several of his romances led to tragedy. His first love, for Daphne, the daughter of the river god, was unreciprocated and came about as a result of Apollo's arrogance. He had sneered at Eros, the god of love, insisting that Eros was a lesser man with a bow and arrow. In retribution, Eros shot a golden love-arrow into Apollo's heart, smiting him with yearning for Daphne. Into Daphne's heart he aimed a love-repelling arrow, which made her flee from Apollo's ardent advances. When he pursued her, she cried to her father for help and was turned into a laurel tree just as Apollo reached her. Apollo made the tree one of his symbols and decorated his hair with wreaths made from the leaves. Today, the laurel wreath symbolises victory and leadership.

Another pursued by Apollo was Cassandra, the daughter of Priam and Hecuba, the king and queen of Troy. Apollo fell in love with Cassandra and, although she did not love him in return, she longed for the gift of prophecy and so agreed to become Apollo's lover in exchange. After he bestowed the gift on her, she refused to keep her side of the bargain. Furious, Apollo ensured that no-one would believe her when she spoke of the future and Cassandra was shut away by her own kind, who considered her to be insane and refused to listen to her.

In relationships, Apollo was mostly cool and detached, choosing strong women who would provide a challenge. But he insisted on being both the centre of attention and the one with the balance of power. His preoccupation with order, and his need to retreat for three months each year, made for an emotional distance that was not an easy quality to have within relationships.

Apollo had three children. Asclepius was the son of Apollo and Coronis. A raven appointed by Apollo to watch over Coronis through her pregnancy told Apollo that she had been unfaithful to him. In a rage, he killed her; then, as her body was placed on the funeral pyre, he regretted his hasty action and rescued Asclepius from her womb. The boy was reared by the centaur Chiron, the healer and tutor to the gods, and Asclepius in turn became the god of healing and medicine. His powers were so great that he could even bring the dead to life. This led to his downfall when Hades, god of the underworld where the shades (souls) of the dead were taken, complained that because of Asclepius' gift his realm was in danger of becoming obsolete. Zeus agreed with Hades that this would not do and killed Asclepius with a thunderbolt. Apollo insisted that his son be set in the heavens as Ophiuchus, the serpent-bearer, so that he could still watch over the Earth.

Another son of Apollo was Aristaeus, who was born through a union with a nymph, Cyrene, and was also brought up by Chiron. He became a healer and visionary and was the protector of flocks and agriculture.

Orpheus was Apollo's son by his liaison with the Muse Calliope. Orpheus was given a lyre by Apollo, who taught him to play it so beautifully that none could resist the music. He fell in love with Eurydice, a nymph, and they were married. But she died from a snakebite and was taken to the underworld realm of Hades. Distraught with grief, Orpheus made his way down to the underworld, knowing that few who went there could return. He calmed the ferryman who took the souls of the dead across the River Styx, and sang the fierce three-headed dog, Cerberus, to sleep in order to gain access to Hades' domain. Once inside, Orpheus pleaded with Hades and Persephone to give him back his wife and they agreed to release her, providing Orpheus did not attempt to look at her until they were back in the realm of the living. However, he was so desperate to see her that he looked back to check that she was following him before they reached the surface, and lost her forever. Each of Apollo's sons, though tragic, was gifted, suggesting the tremendous creative and generative power of the Sun.

Sibling Rivalry

Although the relationship between Apollo and Artemis was close, they enjoyed pitting their formidable wits against each other. Both were superlative archers, and Apollo jealously plotted to get rid of Artemis' lover, Orion, through capitalising on her competitive streak. Pointing out a distant dot on the Ocean, he tricked her into shooting a silver arrow at it. Artemis rose to the challenge, only to discover afterwards that she had killed her lover. Distraught, she placed him in the sky as the constellation Orion, accompanied by one of her dogs, Sirius.

Hermes, Apollo's younger half-brother, was the son of Zeus and Maia, whose Titan father, Atlas, carried the world on his shoulders. On the day that Hermes was born he invented the lyre, then stole some prized cattle from Apollo. Disguising his footsteps with branches, he drove fifty of Apollo's cattle backwards, thinking that his trick would not be discovered. Apollo, however, saw through the ploy and confronted Hermes, who by then had roasted and eaten two cows and was pretending to be asleep in his mother's cave. Although Hermes at first denied any involvement, eventually he agreed to exchange his lyre for the stolen cattle and was allowed to keep the remaining forty-eight cows.

Apollo's music followed the laws of harmony and logic. Not for him was the wild abandon of gods such as Dionysus. Apollo's music was ordered and clear. The relationship between music and mathematics is very Apollonian. He strove to create sounds that calmed the heart and soothed away the wilder emotions; that evoked a sense of purity of spirit.

Archetypal Resonance

Apollo as an archetype embodies the ability to see clearly and to understand what he sees. His gaze is far-reaching and all-encompassing. He is the arrow that drives straight to the heart of the goal. He is the maker and upholder of laws. The overview is more important to him than the details, as he looks at how the whole will be affected, rather than the components that make up the whole. The Apollo archetype is the master of control, of logical thought processes and clear, concise assessment and judgement. Thinking is more important than feeling; the mind rules over the emotions, though he is susceptible to flattery because of his sense of pride. Order and harmony are important to him. Knowledge is his primary concern, as this brings understanding, growth and expansion. As the favourite son, he embodies the need and the expectation to shine among the company of others. When this element of Apollo's nature is fulfilled, the archetype truly comes into his own, and his benevolence is experienced as a warm glow that radiates far beyond his immediate sphere.

The Qualities of the Sun

The Sun, a young star in its prime, shines high above us, unaffected by our human viewpoints and considerations. Born around 4.6 billion years ago from a swirling molecular cloud of gases and expected to survive in its present state for at least a further 5 billion years, the Sun is fuelled by nuclear energy that is generated from deep within its core. There is no solid rock on the Sun – it is gaseous from the surface to the core. The light that emanates from its surface only gives clues as to the inner temperatures and is strong enough to illuminate the far reaches of the solar system.

As the centre of our solar system and our source of life, the Sun casts light on the Earth, vivifies, makes all things visible, reveals and defines the shapes and forms that it illuminates. The areas where the Sun shines brightest contain the deepest shadows as contrasts are picked out and clarified. The Sun symbolises knowledge, birth, growth, creativity, order, logic and spiritual illumination. Nothing can be hidden from the Sun's eye; it sees all and ultimately judges nothing. The Sun warms the earth and facilitates growth, but too much of an exposure to it burns fertile earth to a wasteland and creates barrenness. It engenders respect. In the winter the strength of the Sun wanes, as Apollo retires to the temporary sanctuary of Hyperborea to gather his energy for the months to come.

In Your Natal Chart

Apollo is a ruling influence in your natal chart, just as he is a powerful force on Olympus. The Sun sign that you are born under provides the lens for your self-expression and shows how you develop and manifest your creative impulses. The Sun, astrologically, represents the core of your being, your true inner nature. Even if other archetypal voices may appear to speak more loudly through your natal chart, the position of the Sun reveals how you experience and express your inner sense of purpose and self-empowerment, and indicates the areas in which you 'shine'.

The Sun rules growth, clear-sightedness, logic, and spiritual as well as temporal understanding. It gives clues as to areas of achievement, attainment and success, and reveals the focus of the inner drive that can be directed towards your goals in life. Confidence, passion and the need to be recognised and acknowledged by others are all denoted by the position of the Sun in your natal chart. There is a sense of immediacy in the area of your chart that the Sun is found in and this is manifested through its position in the astrological sign and the house that it lies in. The Sun insists on expressing itself – even when it is hidden behind a cloud, its influence is felt. Aspects to the Sun take these insights further and reveal the relationships between the different archetypal forces that resonate within you. The aspects also indicate whether the positive or negative qualities of those archetypes are being brought into play, and give a clearer perspective on how to best work with these influences. If you are expressing Apollonian qualities to the detriment of other areas of the self — so your thinking is ruling strongly over feeling — then Apollo is ruling you rather than being just one element of the psyche. Where the Sun is concerned, this can help you to gauge which qualities of Apollo are ruling you, rather than being ruled by you. The power principle that the Sun governs may be obvious and outwardly dynamic in the natal chart, or may lie deeper beneath the surface, depending on its position.

The influence of Apollo is felt through your need to have a goal to aim for. The bow and arrow of Apollo's intent must have a target; otherwise it can turn against itself and be expressed as self-destructive impulses. Apollo's ability to see clearly, to set aside any emotional considerations in favour of logic, reason and forethought, casts light on areas that may be missed or ignored if the emotions are running high. Your powers of judgement are gifts bestowed by Apollo and these stem from an inner urge towards rightness and morality.

There is a competitive element in the Sun. This derives from Apollo's need and desire always to be first: to be the favoured son, the sought-after lover, the voice of reason, the fount of knowledge. The Sun, like Apollo, must be the brightest luminary in the sky.

Rulership of the Sun

The Sun governs the astrological sign Leo. Leos are gregarious, generous with their resources, whether time, energy, money or affection; creative and magnanimous, especially when others are around to notice. The symbol for Leo, the Lion, has a mane that is similar to the rays of the Sun and is known as the king of beasts. Statues of Apollo are easily recognised by his beautiful physique and halo of curly hair, which is reminiscent of the Sun's rays.

The qualities of Apollo are at their most pronounced in Leos. His role as the favourite son is often played out through this sign, as Leos thrive on praise, and will actively seek it out. Apollo's skill and determination are apparent in the Sun's rulership of Leo, as is his ability to be the one in power who delegates with flair and aplomb. Apollo as patron of the oracle at Delphi did not need the actual skills of prophecy. His charisma was such that others would carry out tasks for him, while he accepted the approbation.

Apollo's retreat to the sanctuary of Hyperborea is reflected in the Leonine love of sunshine and a place to stretch out, catlike, and relax. This also satisfies the need for a change in routine and provides the space for allowing an influx of creative ideas. The outgoing, active nature of the Sun expresses itself most positively when it is balanced by periods of leisure and the renewal of a connection with the spiritual self.

When the Sun holds a prominent position in the natal chart, or is strongly aspected by other planets, issues connected with the will, desires or ego can be dominant. Apollo felt compelled always to be first and best, and sought this through his roles of the favourite son and the brightest luminary in the sky. There can be a tendency to dominate because of this, which can be tempered through finding positive outlets for expression that naturally result in praise and respect from others.

The Apollonian sense of drama is apparent in strong Sun aspects. This can result in abundant creativity and talented acting and role-playing. There is such a strong charisma that others will gravitate to it to become part of the charmed circle of which the Sun is the centre. Even in his relationship with his siblings, Apollo liked to be centre stage and revelled in creating scenes that would be remarked on.

The Sun's warmth draws us towards it. Yet its benevolence hides a certain detachment. The Sun shines on all, regardless of status or circumstance, and is close to few; it is set apart from others by its very nature. Attempt to move too close and you could be burned. Respect it, and you will grow and flourish in its light.

CHAPTER THREE

The Moon ☽
Artemis/Diana

The archetype of the virgin goddess defines the essential qualities of Artemis. Contrary to the modern perception of a virgin as one who is not sexually awakened, the true meaning of this term is 'untouched, complete within oneself'. Artemis (along with Athena and Hestia) retains the secret, mysterious aspects of herself. She is aware of her own innate sense of wholeness, and she does not seek approbation from others; she is true to her own instincts, drives and desires. Artemis follows her own course, and accepts the consequences of her decisions and actions.

Because of this inner integrity, the virgin goddess archetype has an inward-looking focus, an ability to recognise motives and act on them, regardless of whether or not these make sense to other people. Artemis goes her own way. She seeks out the solitude that enables her to feel connected to the natural world, and that enables her to define herself in her own eyes and not through the eyes of others. She is self-sufficient, self-contained, self-assured.

The Birth of Artemis

Twin sister to Apollo, and the firstborn, Artemis immediately supported her mother, Leto, and acted as midwife during the long and arduous birth of her brother. This earned her the roles of goddess of childbirth and of the Moon, the planet that strongly influences the menstrual cycles of women. Whereas Apollo was given over into the care of Themis, Artemis stayed with her mother and took on a protective role. When she was brought before her father, Zeus, the king of the gods, he was so impressed by her that he offered her any gift that she wished for. Artemis chose a silver bow and arrows (the metal associated with the Moon), a pack of hounds, and a band of nymphs who would live in the wilderness with her. Her requests were granted.

Artemis the Protectress

Artemis is the protector of women, particularly during childbirth, and always answered pleas for help with swift, sometimes merciless, action. She rescued her mother from an attempted rape by a giant, Tityus, and killed him. When the goddess Niobe slighted Leto, Artemis and Apollo took their revenge by hunting down and killing Niobe's children, Artemis killing her six daughters, and Apollo her six sons, before turning Niobe into a pillar of stone.

The dark side of the Moon, the private side that never turns its face to the light of the Sun and the eyes of those on Earth, is also the domain of Artemis. She loved the dark and would hunt by moonlight and the light of torches. No man was allowed to spy on her or her nymphs, and any who attempted to do so met with immediate punishment. When the hunter Actaeon stumbled across Artemis and her nymphs bathing and could not resist watching, Artemis turned him into a stag that was pursued and brought down by his own dogs.

Artemis and her nymphs formed a sisterhood that is echoed in modern times whenever women come together with a common aim, whether at leisure or in protest. This mutual support is beneficial to all, and is encompassing and protective. The underlying purpose is self-empowerment and self-exploration in the open and accepting company of other women. Men are excluded from this Artemisian domain, though not from the outward lives of the goddess or the women who seek to embody aspects of her. This sense of female community acts as a foundation for the outer lives of relationships and work. The urge to walk in moonlight and starlight, to be alone in the countryside and woods, to bathe in a stream or pool, unobserved, springs from the Artemisian qualities deep within us.

Relationships

The great love of Artemis was Orion, a mortal hunter, who died as a result of Apollo's jealousy. Angry that his sister's affection was directed towards another man, Apollo watched Orion swim out to sea and plotted his revenge. When Orion was only a distant speck in the water, Apollo sought out Artemis and challenged her to hit the tiny dark shape floating far away in the distance. Unable to resist an opportunity to show off her prowess with the bow and arrow, Artemis aimed true, and Orion was killed. When she discovered that she had been tricked and that her lover was dead, she mourned him deeply and set him in the sky as the constellation Orion, accompanied by her faithful hound, Sirius.

Artemis' love of solitude, her desire to be among a select band of trusted women, and her role as protector of women in need (whose pleas for help came through their associations with men) took precedence over romantic relationships. And indeed, men were in awe of her, even afraid of her. Her strength, skill and containment could be intimidating to males, especially those who felt emasculated by women who were a law unto themselves and who needed nothing from others. The nature of the Moon reflects this – a partner of the Sun, a friend of the dark, apparently cool and detached while also capable of bringing the emotions of others to the surface.

Archetypal Resonance

Artemis as an archetype embodies the independent free-thinker. She is determined to do things her way, and find all that she needs within herself. Relationships are of secondary importance, as they draw her attention outwards rather than inwards, and distract her from the goals that are her primary consideration.

Artemis embodies the ability to be fully focused. Nothing can distract her once a decision has been made. The Artemis archetype revels in competition, because this spurs on the motivational impulses and creates a longed-for challenge. There is a sense of community with other women, a singularity of vision and purpose, and an attunement to the realms of the hidden and mysterious.

The call of the wilderness is especially strong within the Artemis archetype, symbolising the need to experience and navigate uncharted domains within ourselves: the hidden, often dark and rocky aspects of our inner nature. The wilderness is where the deep self resides, the wild untamed self that is expressed through instinct and intuition which leads us towards hidden truths.

The Qualities of the Moon

The Moon is estimated to be almost as old as our solar system, indicating that it was formed in the early stages of the planetary formations. Moon rocks brought back from Apollo XVI and subjected to analysis estimate their age to be around 4 million to 4.5 million years.

The Moon is scarred by meteorites, and its terrain consists of vast plains and mountain ranges. Its atmosphere has long since evaporated, but in the darkest areas where sunlight cannot reach are pools of water in the form of ice.

The rulership of the Moon by Artemis reveals the subtle, changeable, reflective side of this archetype. Moonlight casts very different shadows than sunlight. The Moon softly illuminates; its glow draws our eyes and evokes deep emotions, whereas the Sun is too bright to be looked upon with the naked eye. Although the Sun appears to dominate the Moon, the phase when Artemis is seen as at her most powerful, the New Moon, is the time when solar eclipses occur. The New Moon then passes between the Earth and the Sun, casting its shadow on the surface of the Earth, and briefly blotting out its sibling.

The Moon, our satellite, is as important to the survival of life on Earth as the Sun. The Moon affects the tides, the water contained within our cells and our blood, and our emotions. Its changing face as it waxes and wanes, guides women through the menstrual cycle, heightens the connection with the instinctual nature when it shows its fullest face, and gives its name to lunacy – the madness that comes through ploughing the depths of the apparently hidden or forbidden.

Dreams are the gift of the Moon, for it shines on us while we sleep, allowing access to the unconscious mind. And just as the Moon appears to die each month, only to be reborn, to generate itself, so are the cells in our bodies repeatedly renewed in order to maintain health.

The cycles of the Moon mirror the cycles of life: birth, growth, death, renewal. We see these cycles reflected in the plant and animal kingdoms in a continuous process that allows evolution to occur. Creativity is an aspect of this – the ability to connect with something deep within the self, and to give birth to new forms as a result. Lovers revere the Moon, as do artists, poets, writers and craftspeople, because it is a continual reminder of the relationship we have with mystery.

In Your Natal Chart

The Moon in your natal chart governs the unconscious mind, the deep emotions, instinct and intuition. This planet rules your emotional responses, and shows how your emotional outlook has been coloured by early experiences. The Moon position reveals your relationship with your mother, and with women in general. Depending upon the astrological sign and house that it is found in, your imaginative visionary faculties and the ability to dream and to use your dreams for self-understanding are activated. The Moon position also reveals issues of safety and security and indicates whether your emotional needs are met. Negative aspects to the Moon tend to show areas of life where you experience a lack of comfort or security. The placement of the Moon indicates in which areas of your life you act out unconscious impulses and pre-conditioned responses, and respond to stimuli, and is also associated with memory. In essence, the Moon in your birth chart is the mirror of your feeling nature.

Just as Artemis is drawn to the wilderness, so does the influence of the Moon provide access to the secrets of the wild self. The inner drive of the Moon is that of allowing change, of understanding that life moves in cycles, and that the deep emotions can provide a powerful impetus for change if they are used positively.

Although the Sun, the bright twin of the Moon, appears initially to be more powerful than its sister, the two are equals — halves of one whole that cannot be separated. The Sun provides the energy for life, but its light, when reflected by the Moon, makes growth and change possible. The feeling, intuitive, dreaming nature that is expressed through your Moon position underpins the outward expression of your personality that is found through your Sun sign.

Positive aspects between the Moon and other planets indicate a constructive ability to feel and express your emotions. They show how we connect to our inner nature and, through this, how we relate to others in an intuitive, compassionate manner. Negative aspects, depending on the planets and houses involved, can manifest as either repressed or suppressed emotions, tense relationships with women, the mother, or public figures, or a predisposition to be driven irrationally by the tides of feeling.

The Moon is the key to our memories and dreams, our fears and our ability to plumb the hidden depths. The influence of Artemis as Moon goddess is felt through the desire to experience the female aspect of the self with power, strength, independence and acceptance.

Rulership of the Moon

The Moon governs the astrological sign Cancer, whose symbol, the Crab, lives out its life under the influences of the tides of the sea as the Moon draws these across the Earth. The sea embodies life, through the emergence of the first creatures from the primeval soup aeons ago. Symbolically, water signifies the emotions and the deep aspects of the psyche.

When the Moon is prominent in your natal chart, you are ruled by your emotional tides, even though you may prefer to hide your sensitivity beneath a tough exterior. Artemis, though strong, proud and independent, cared deeply for those close to her, and was fiercely protective. She needed the company of her nymphs, with its attendant sense of community and belonging. But, as with her twin, Apollo, she also sought solitude, though for her it was the wild places that renewed and replenished her. When her privacy was infringed upon, she could be merciless but, if allowed a period of seclusion, the company of kindred spirits was welcomed and celebrated.

Children of the Moon are complex creatures, reluctant to be known too familiarly. They crave security and build strong, sometimes impenetrable, defences in order to hide their feelings of vulnerability. Like their archetype, they set their sights high, though they prefer to aim at what is attainable rather than take unnecessary risks. Competitiveness arises from a need to prove themselves, and to hide their gentle side, as they fear scorn more than anything. Like Artemis, they have a connection with the wild self, and an urge to seek out places of solitude and safety.

In relationships, possessiveness can become an issue, and this can prove detrimental. In the story of Artemis and Orion, the goddess was tricked into killing her lover because the relationship was excluding Apollo, and he was jealous that a mere mortal had all the attention that he felt should be his. The influence of the Moon, when strongly felt in the natal chart, can exert a powerful, all-encompassing pull on the emotions that can be difficult to deal with both for the loved one and for others.

The Artemis archetype, when heard above the other elements in the psyche, is not willing to compromise, and refuses to listen to opinions that do not conform with their own. Yet there is an innate understanding of human nature, and a profound sympathy and empathy for those in need of help.

The Moon's glow is subtle, casting a cool, gentle radiance. It allows that which is hidden to remain hidden, and does not pry or demand.

CHAPTER FOUR

Mercury ☿
Hermes

The essential quality of Hermes is communication. The need to satisfy curiosity, the urge to forge links between others is a fundamental aspect of this god. The dual nature of both the deity and the planet is reflected through the modes of communication that are expressed according to mood. Hermes embodies the exchange of ideas, the stimulation of the quicksilver aspects of the mind. This can occur through verbal and written interchange, through a search for understanding, or through mischief-making designed to confuse others and provide Hermes with entertainment at their expense.

The epitome of adolescence, with its alternating boyish charm and hidden barbs, defines Hermes archetypally. Yet beneath this rests an urge to be of use. He is also the guide, the deity who alone has the skill to escort the souls of the dead from the light down to the underworld, the realm of Hades; to forge links between the conscious mind and the shadowy depths of the unconscious.

The Birth of Hermes

Maia, the mother of Hermes, managed to escape retribution from Hera, as Zeus seduced her while Hera was asleep. A daughter of Atlas, the Titan who supported the heavens on his shoulders, Maia lived in the Pleiades constellation and was a quiet and retiring luminary.

Hermes, like the other deities, sprang into action as soon as he left his mother's womb. He immediately set about making mischief. Within a few hours of birth, he invented the lyre, using the shell of a tortoise as the body of the instrument, and adding strings. The music he made soothed and uplifted all who heard it. On the same day, intent on annoying his half-brother Apollo, he stole Apollo's prized cattle and, when found out, was forced by an angry Zeus to hand over his lyre to Apollo in exchange, and transfer with it the title of god of music. Hermes' role as mischief-maker and trickster was set in place from birth, and he enjoyed creating havoc and playing tricks on his siblings.

Personality Traits

Hermes was fun-loving, quick-thinking and inventive. He could be immature and childlike, and his appearance was eternally youthful, but he was also deceptive and manipulative, with no compunction about being creative with the truth. Truth, to Hermes, was easily twisted if that would bring about the results he desired. This trickster element in his nature made it possible for him to see through the machinations of others and to find the kernel that always lay at the heart of the matter, in order to turn situations to his advantage. Hermes was an opportunist, yet one who was always ready to take on the role of guide – both through the labyrinthine corridors of the mind and through physical terrain.

Winged sandals and helmet enabled him to travel swiftly and far, between the lofty heights of Mount Olympus, the Earth and the underworld. His totem metal, quicksilver, reflects his mercurial qualities and his ability to shift instantly from one mode of thinking or physical place to another. This changeable aspect of his nature made him unpredictable, and not always popular with members of his family whose attitudes were more fixed. Hermes could not be pinned down. His approach was that of a shape-shifter, who can change form in an instant, though this form was mental rather than physical. Yet he had a natural, easy charm that convinced those whom he had offended to forgive him after a cooling-off period.

The Messenger

Hermes' eloquence gave him a natural role as the god of speech and communication, and he became the messenger of the gods. He protected travellers, athletes and thieves, and was considered to bring good fortune to those whom he favoured. A master wordsmith himself, he invented the alphabet and bequeathed the gift of writing to mortals, becoming a favourite of writers and public speakers.

As messenger, he interceded between gods and mortals and also acted as a guide for souls travelling to the underworld realm, ruled by Hades, after death. He carried a caduceus, a staff entwined with two snakes and topped with wings, which denoted his position as herald of the gods and was used for healing, as well as marking him out as a being of knowledge and authority. The caduceus, as an alchemical symbol, represents the union of the male and female elements of the psyche and signifies death and rebirth, sexuality and procreation through its similarity to the structure of DNA in the body. Hermes is associated with magic and is often depicted as the Magician in the tarot.

He could be kind and helpful, and came to the aid of Demeter and Persephone when Hades abducted Persephone and took her into the underworld to be his wife (the full story of Demeter and Persephone is told in Chapter 13). When Persephone was released from the underworld, Hermes acted as her guide and took her back to a joyful reunion with her mother.

Relationships

Hermes had many liaisons and was reputed to be bisexual, but his mercurial nature meant that it was impossible for his lovers to pin him down and extract promises of commitment. His longest-lived affair was with Aphrodite, and their union brought about a child, Hermaphroditus, who, as well as being named after both parents, carried the gender qualities of both male and female.

All of the children of Hermes were unusual. Pan, who was half-man and half-goat, became the god of the woods and shepherds. His bawdy, wild, lustful nature and his cloven hooves became associated with the Christian view of the devil, and the words 'panic' and 'pandemonium' stemmed from his influence. Another aspect to Pan, however, was the ability to bring about states of ecstasy through playing his pan-pipes. All who heard this would be charmed.

Eudorus, another son, embodied Hermes' most positive traits, and devoted himself to caring for his flocks and those who came into contact with him. Autolycus took on his father's least appealing traits, and was shunned as an untrustworthy thief and liar. Myrtilus was amoral to the extent of homicide. Each of Hermes' children reflected and magnified the many unpredictable qualities of their father.

Sibling Rivalry

As a younger brother, Hermes resented occupying what he considered to be a lowly position in the Olympian pecking order and enjoyed baiting his siblings. His arch-rival was Apollo, the golden one, whom Zeus made no secret of favouring. Hermes' theft of Apollo's cattle set the relationship off to a rocky start, as although he achieved his aim of keeping the prize, he was taken before Zeus, who was not fooled by his protested innocence and demanded that Hermes' lyre be given to Apollo in exchange.

Relationships with his other siblings were, on the whole, harmonious, as Hermes was gregarious, fun-loving and communicative. His willingness to be a messenger between the gods, and on their behalf with mortals, made him useful to the family, even though they were aware that his propensity for mischief did not always render him entirely trustworthy. Hermes always had an eye open for the main chance and took the opportunity to grasp it when he could. But his intelligence, and his ability to make fun of himself as well as others was endearing.

Archetypal Resonance

Hermes as an archetype embodies the urge to communicate and to forge connections both intellectually and physically. The mercurial aspect of the mind is capable of gaining insights through taking leaps across spaces between divergent ideas, in much the same way as electrical impulses surge through the neural pathways in the brain and enable connections to be made that were not previously apparent. This swift changeability can be the stuff of inspiration and innovation but, on the negative side, can lead to confused thinking. The process of accelerated thinking can be utilised both creatively and deceptively, and reflects the shifting facets of the Hermes archetype. Within this, there is a necessary choice as to whether that facility is used positively or negatively, as the flashes of genius that result are not bound by moral codes or a need to seek approbation from others.

As an archetype, Hermes represents the messenger, the necessity for communication that links together thoughts, ideas and words. Sociability is an integral part of this as in order to communicate there must be someone to communicate with or to, and the Hermes archetype needs the company of others in which to shine.

Another archetypal aspect of Hermes is that of rescuer. The Hermes mindset wants to help others, and enjoys being useful and needed, as long as a solution can be found quickly and acted on. The urge for constant change means that the new is always welcomed — too much continuity leads to boredom, and so the Hermes archetype is always in search of new experiences. Information is treasured both for its power and for its use in creating increased connections. Intelligence is highly valued, as stimulation is vital.

The Qualities of Mercury

Mercury is a small planet, the closest to the Sun in our solar system. It is so close that a block of lead would melt instantly in the vicinity of the side of the planet that turns its face towards the Sun. Yet the dark side of Mercury is unimaginably cold — about minus 180 degrees Celsius. This dual nature tells us a great deal about the extraordinary character of the planet, the archetype and the astrological interpretation. The metal mercury, also known as quicksilver, is unique because it does not behave as other metals do. One of its uses is in thermometers, and it enables temperature to be measured accurately, just as Hermes is sensitive to, and quick to ascertain, the mental and emotional moods and temperature of those around him. However, break the thermometer, and set the mercury free, and it immediately divides into numerous globules that run in all directions and are difficult to pin down and contain.

The proximity of the planet Mercury to the Sun reveals indications as to the relationship between Hermes and Apollo. The siblings blow hot and cold, yet are inextricably bound together.

In Your Natal Chart

Mercury indicates how you think and communicate, and these processes are reflected through the astrological sign in which the planet is situated. This reveals your ability to make decisions and deductions, to forge connections and utilise these. The house position in your chart shows the area of life that is most influenced by the information that you gather.

Aspects between Mercury and the other planets give information as to how the intellect is used and what mode of communication is most natural to you. The aspects can indicate whether mental energy is swift or sluggish, free-flowing or easily blocked. The planet's close proximity to the Sun means that Mercury's position in the natal chart is never far from that of the Sun. When it rests at its closest point to its sibling, Mercury's effect is intensified, bequeathing either moments of brilliance and insight that can change your mindset and those of others; or, conversely, mental burn-out.

Self-expression is vital to Mercury. When this flows freely through other elements in the natal chart, communication is speedy and clear. If this is blocked, there is muddled speech and thinking, and frustration due to the inability to communicate ideas and words clearly to others.

Intellectual pursuits and hobbies, interests and activities are attributed to Mercury, and so are relationships with siblings, friends and neighbours and colleagues, which reflect Hermes' sociability. The house that Mercury is found in also indicates short journeys and attitudes towards education.

The trickster element of Hermes is reflected in the planetary position, which gives pointers as to whether this is used mischievously, as in a fun-loving character, manipulatively, as in a likeable rogue, or maliciously, as in a con artist. Mercury, like Hermes, needs outlets through which to channel constructive self-expression.

Rulership of Mercury

Mercury rules the astrological signs of Gemini and Virgo. Its expression is different within each sign, reflecting the changeable aspects of both the planet and the archetype. Gemini is symbolised by the Twins, with their attributes of a dual nature, quick-wittedness, hasty speech and shifting moods. Communication is all-important for Geminis, and their sense of fun and constant flow of bright ideas make them very popular. The Gemini mind is versatile and non-conformist; stimulation is necessary, because Geminis become bored easily and when this happens they will create mischief in order to shift the status quo. A keen, open mind and adaptability makes them fascinating companions, though sometimes elusive and unpredictable. Hermes' charm is very apparent in this sign and they make friends easily, though tend to move on when someone new or more stimulating appears.

Mercury's rulership of Virgo reflects other aspects of the planetary archetype. Whereas Gemini absorbs information like a sponge, skimming the surface intellectually in order to pursue many diverse topics, and uses this information for creating connections with others in a social sense, Virgo's thirst for knowledge is more selective and is directed more inwardly. The Virgoan nature investigates more deeply and is keen to constantly delve beneath the surface. Just as Hermes took on the role of messenger and helpmate to both gods and mortals, Mercury, through its Virgoan aspect, is keen to be of assistance to others. To this end, Virgo focuses intelligence on practical matters, with the aim of bringing ideas to useful fruition. Communication is geared towards work-related ideas and subjects, and service to others, and Virgo is a willing listener.

Hermes' caduceus, with healing as one of its symbolic attributes, is more apparent in the rulership of Virgo, who tends to be health-oriented, views the body as the temple of the soul and is diligent about hygiene and nurturing.

In relationships, the Hermes connection is apparent in Gemini through a natural flirtatiousness and a sense of pleasure in the frisson of new encounters, tempered by a reluctance to be pinned down prematurely. The Virgo aspect of Hermes is more reticent, less swayed by adventure, with communication and conversation as the key to gaining interest. The relationship between Hermes and

Aphrodite, with its ongoing friendship even after the affair was over, is typical of both astrological signs, as is the birth of Hermaphroditus – the offspring that results from the meeting of both mind and body.

Mercury's fluency is determined by its quicksilver nature. The expression of understanding, adaptation and innovation acts as a key to the subtle messages of other archetypes in the psyche and the natal chart, and can indicate which of those speak most strongly through your personality.

CHAPTER FIVE

Venus ♀
Aphrodite

The role of goddess of love credits Aphrodite with less than her due respect. She is the spark that ignites the inner flame of those whom she touches, and transforms the internal and external perspective. Love can be vivifying or destructive; it can suffuse the entire world with beauty, or it can open portals to grief and despair. The true gift of Aphrodite is the transformation that occurs when she steps to the fore in the psyche.

Aphrodite reminds us that we are not solitary islands drifting through an uncaring world. Her power is that of a connecting emotional force that draws us towards one another and enables us to temporarily see with the eyes of a god or goddess. Through her we shift and change, and become more than we were.

The Birth of Aphrodite

There are two versions of Aphrodite's birth. In one, she was the daughter of Zeus and a sea nymph, Dione. In the other, more celebrated story, she emerged from the foam created by the genitals of Uranus when Cronus severed them and cast them into the sea. Botticelli depicts this in his painting *The Birth of Venus,* as she rises above the waves on a giant seashell and is escorted to Mount Olympus by Eros, god of love, and Himeros, god of desire.

The second version of Aphrodite's birth adds to the numinous mystique of the goddess of love and beauty and carries deep symbolic resonance. The combination of sexual desire, which drove Uranus to his painful fate when he approached Gaia, the life-supporting properties of the sea, and the presence of the archetypes of love and desire at her birth created a being whose passions were capable of setting alight the inner spark of all that she touched. By her very nature, she was destined to embody love, creation and inspiration.

Personality Traits

Aphrodite, when honoured, was the epitome of benevolence. She favoured both gods and mortals and had no compunction about using her powers to enchant and, in some cases, to punish. Her positive attributes embody the intense, all-encompassing joy of loving and being loved; of engendering a feeling of passion in the creative process and a profligacy in procreation. Her beauty inspired others to access the loftiest heights of the imagination and create works of art that would endure – whether through the visual arts, drama, dance or the written word. She was helpful towards those who petitioned her, and could transform lives in an instant. One of her devotees was Melanion, a mortal who fell in love with Atalanta, a woman to be reckoned with.

Atalanta was beautiful, and was desired by many, but she was fiercely independent and reluctant to marry any of her suitors. Eventually she declared that any man who could beat her in a race could have her hand in marriage. As she was the fastest runner among mortals and the penalty for losing the race was death, Melanion appealed to Aphrodite to intercede, and the goddess advised him to challenge Atalanta to a race. While they ran, with Atalanta far ahead, Aphrodite threw three golden apples in

Atalanta's path. Their beauty was such that Atalanta paused to pick them up, and Melanion won the race and his bride.

Aphrodite was malicious when not honoured. She was proud of her beauty and sensitive to slights. Often her revenge was directed at her antagonist through an innocent person. Theseus was a hero whom Aphrodite helped, but he paid dearly for betraying her.

The wife of Minos, the king of Crete, fell in love with one of his bulls and birthed a monstrous creature, half-man and half-bull, called the Minotaur. Minos had a labyrinth built to contain the creature and sacrificed young men and women to him each year. Aphrodite enlisted the help of Ariadne, the daughter of King Minos, and was promised by Theseus that he would marry Ariadne after he killed the Minotaur. Ariadne gave Theseus a ball of golden thread that would help him find his way back from the centre of the labyrinth, and a sword with which to slay the Minotaur. His task accomplished, Theseus sailed away from Crete with Ariadne, but refused to marry her, and abandoned her on the deserted island of Dia (now Naxos), where she was later rescued by Dionysus. Theseus married Hippolyta, queen of the Amazons, but she died after giving birth to their son, Hippolytus. Aphrodite bided her time and when Theseus later married Phaedra, Aphrodite caused the unfortunate woman to fall in love with Hippolytus, her stepson. Spurned by him when she declared her feelings, Phaedra hanged herself, leaving a note for Theseus claiming that Hippolytus had attempted to rape her. Theseus, in his fury, called on Poseidon, god of the sea, to destroy his son, and Poseidon sent a wave to drag him into the depths. Afterwards, Theseus discovered the truth and was filled with remorse.

As patroness of love, Aphrodite lights an inner flame and fans it through the meeting of two people whose destinies are interwoven, for good or ill. The love she inspires can elevate or destroy, and the influence of Aphrodite can create a sense of belonging, or terrible unconsummated yearnings.

The Transformer

Aphrodite could bring about self-knowledge and self-empowerment. In the story of Eros and Psyche, the seeming revenge of the goddess brings unexpected results.

Psyche was a beautiful mortal who inadvertently offended Aphrodite because men compared her beauty favourably with that of the goddess. Aphrodite sent Eros to make Psyche fall in love with a creature of great ugliness. But Eros fell in love with Psyche and took her away with him, commanding her not to attempt to look upon his face. Psyche, understandably curious, lit a candle while Eros was sleeping, but a drop of tallow fell on the god and he woke and flew away. In despair, Psyche appealed to Aphrodite, who gave her four impossible tasks to accomplish in order to be reunited with Eros.

The first task was to sort a mountain of mixed seeds into separate heaps. The second was to gather fleece from the terrifying golden rams of the Sun. The third was to fill a flask with water from an inaccessible stream and the fourth was to take a casket to Persephone in the underworld and bring it back filled with beauty ointment. Psyche received unexpected help and through fulfilling the tasks she won both Eros as her husband and the status of goddess.

Relationships

Aphrodite had numerous lovers among both gods and mortals. She was married to Hephaestus, the crippled son of Zeus and Hera, whose imperfection so offended his mother at birth that she threw him down to Earth from the heights of Mount Olympus. Hephaestus lived among mortals and built a deserved reputation as a master craftsman and smith. He created artefacts of such irresistible beauty that he was in great demand. Aphrodite was constantly unfaithful to him and included Hermes, Ares and Dionysus among her immortal lovers. Of the mortals, Adonis was her favourite, though Persephone loved him also. When Adonis died, Zeus decreed that he should spend one-third of his time alone, one-third with Persephone and one-third with Aphrodite.

The goddess bore children by several of her lovers. Among them were Hermaphroditus, her child by Hermes, the fierce twins Deimos and Phobos (Fear and Panic), and a daughter, Harmonia, by Ares. In Roman myths, Eros (Cupid) is her son, though the Greeks viewed him as a primal god who came into being at the beginning.

Aphrodite was governed by her passions and this humiliated and infuriated Hephaestus. Outwardly they appeared mismatched, yet both had extraordinary creative powers and, despite her unfaithfulness, they remained together. Aphrodite's flaunting of her liaison with Ares so enraged Hephaestus that he decided to embarrass the lovers publicly. He created a net of such fine mesh that none could see it and trapped his wife and her lover within it in mid-coitus, then called all of the gods to come and witness what he hoped would be their shame. However, the plan backfired. The gods found the situation hilarious and laughed so much that Hephaestus was forced to free the pair. The charm of Aphrodite was irresistible.

Sibling Rivalry

Her willingness to be of help made Aphrodite much loved by gods, goddesses and mortals. Her sparkling enthusiasm for life and love, and her extraordinary beauty, made it hard as well as unwise for others to deliberately cross her.

Among the family of Olympians, Hera was Aphrodite's main opponent. Aphrodite's casual attitude towards relationships and marriage antagonised the older goddess, whose domain was the sanctity of marriage despite her husband's frequent infidelity. Hera's strong moral codes were anathema to Aphrodite's urge to flow with the moment and take skilful advantage of opportunities. But Aphrodite ignored Hera, viewed her as a victim of her own strong morals, and put the other goddess's attitude down to jealousy.

Archetypal Resonance

Aphrodite as an archetype embodies the urge towards union. This manifests as the desire to give and receive love and to experience a sense of merging with the beloved. When we are in love, everything and everyone appears beautiful. The world is suffused with a rosy glow, and others sense the radiance around us even if they do not see it, and are drawn towards it like moths to a flame. The world loves lovers. Beauty is perceived even in the mundane, because Aphrodite sees through our eyes and experiences through our heightened senses. In the first flush of love we become god and goddess in the eyes of the loved one.

This desire to experience unity, when not expressed through a physical relationship, is found in artistic, creative people when an idea strikes that fires a passionate response. A painting, a series of dance steps, a poem, a manuscript all arise through a connection with Aphrodite when that creative act becomes an extension of the creator. The work that results in manifesting the idea is viewed as joyful rather than arduous, even when that work is complex. During the creative process, time loses all meaning except for the act of grasping what is available for the task in hand.

The yearning for harmony and warmth so fundamental to our well-being is an aspect of the Aphrodite archetype. Focus is another – the intense focus that 'tunes out' all distractions during a conversation or the undertaking of an act that brings pleasure. The Aphrodite archetype shuns boredom and wishes only to experience pleasure. Monotony drives her deep within the psyche, allowing other archetypes to raise their voices until something beautiful captures the attention, when she rises once more and brings a glow to the world.

The Qualities of Venus

Venus is the second planet from the Sun; a hot, radiant globe surrounded by impenetrable clouds. The 'greenhouse effect' on Venus reflects the heat that is generated by passion, which makes the object of desire unknowable even as we strain to understand them. It is caused by volcanoes on the surface that erupt and expel sulphur dioxide, blocking the light of the Sun and making the planet luminous from the outside but dark beneath the cloud layers. This returns to the surface as rain composed of undiluted sulphuric acid. The atmospheric pressures are immense, and temperatures hover at around 465 degrees Celsius. Symbolically, the fires of love, when entered into, are all-consuming.

As the brightest of the planets, Venus is easily seen with the naked eye and is often known as the 'Morning Star'. The beauty and luminosity of the planet draws the eye, and lovers wish upon it for blessings and good fortune.

In Your Natal Chart

Venus in the natal chart reveals your emotional temperature in relationships with others. Your sense of beauty and harmony stems from Venus, as does artistic and romantic self-expression. The astrological sign that Venus is found in acts as a mirror for how you experience and express your feelings and reveals your approach towards possessions, comfort and the arts. The house in which Venus sits shows your modes of expression through that particular area of life. Whether Venus brings intense passions, as in the sign of Scorpio, or an altruistic love of humanity, as in Pisces, the reverberations from this planet are strongly felt.

Aspects between Venus and other planets show whether the emotions are allowed free rein or are stifled by other planets, other voices in the psyche. Positive aspects reflect the enchanting side of Aphrodite, through an openness to create love, beauty and harmony all around. Challenging aspects can stultify the emotions, creating coldness or manipulation, or can over-exaggerate reactions and reveal hypersensitivity, laziness, or obsession.

Feeling is imperative to Venus and to Aphrodite. When there is freedom to feel and express the emotions, the goddess brings her attributes of charm and liveliness to the fore. Blocked emotions, or feelings of being neglected or undervalued, cause the goddess to go to ground in the subconscious mind and lead to resentment, loss of self-worth and depression.

Rulership of Venus

Venus rules the astrological signs of Taurus and Libra. Both express a desire for beauty and harmony around them and both have an intensely sensual, loving nature. Aphrodite's expression through the earthy, physical aspect of Taurus reveals itself in an appreciation of all things that appeal to the senses. Soft fabrics and skin, delightful scents, appetising food and drink, and melodious voices all call to the Taurean sensitivities. Appearances, values and possessions, especially those with attractive shapes and forms, are important to Taureans, who are miserable when surrounded by what they perceive as ugliness. The Taurean nature is drawn to items that are pleasing to touch and look at and they have a keen eye for beauty.

The emotional nature of Aphrodite lies beneath the surface in Taureans, and their reluctance to appear vulnerable can hold them back from expressing their feelings too openly until they are sure that these will be reciprocated. When they feel secure, they can be a rock for others to lean on, but they can also be possessive, wanting to keep what they love – people and possessions – close to their reach. Like Aphrodite, Taureans are loyal to those who cleave to them, and are generous, giving a great deal of themselves in friendships and relationships.

The strong Taurean willpower makes them able to set a goal and plan far into the future, just as Aphrodite, once she devised a plan or scheme, was willing to wait patiently for the most effective time to take action. The story of Aphrodite and Theseus is a case in point, as she was willing to wait for years to wreak her revenge on Theseus through his family. Similarly, Taureans may not act immediately if they are offended or displeased, but will bide their time until the moment comes when their actions will have the most impact.

Pleasure in indulging the senses is typical of Taureans. Quality is more important than quantity and no expense is spared when Taureans seek to impress, or seduce the object of their desires.

When shining through the lens of her rulership of Libra, Aphrodite's love of harmony and luxury is pronounced. The goddess often bestows on Librans the qualities of physical attractiveness, a delight in pleasure and a need to be liked and loved by others. Approval and popularity are all-important to that sign, just as they are to Aphrodite. Her willingness to help when petitioned is also pronounced in this sign, and her patronage of the arts flows through both Taurus and Libra. Often, Taureans will have beautiful voices, and Librans will have a natural affinity for artistic and creative pursuits that enable them to indulge a love of beauty while simultaneously experiencing a sense of union through the creative process.

The Libran connection with Saturn, through that planet's exaltation in this sign, fosters a strong sense of justice, represented by the scales that are symbolised on the Libran glyph. Fairness is imperative and, as with Aphrodite and Ariadne, they can be crusaders for a particular cause.

New ideas, intellectual stimulation and a love of creating connections with other people make Librans sociable and delightful company. But they find it difficult to make decisions because they can see both sides of a choice or situation and tend to waver while they consider which is best. As with the scales that go up and down according to the weight of their contents, the Libran has to strive to attain balance and equilibrium. Like Taureans, they prefer a peaceful life to emotional upheaval but, when crossed, both signs are capable of dire acts of retribution. Relationships are vital to well-being. Emotional discord can make them physically ill, whereas harmony around them and the attention of a loved one creates a glow that spreads out to encompass all who come close.

CHAPTER SIX

Mars
Ares

Ares embodies the impulses that call out to be followed, no matter what consequences arise. His energy, when channelled, gives rise to immense drive and achievement. The urge to action makes him hasty in speech and deed and, if left to its own devices with no specific goal in mind, turns on itself and those around.

With this archetype there are no sly twists and turns, or convoluted machinations. Ares is the skater on the surface of life, unconcerned about checking first whether the ice is strong enough to hold his weight as he hurries to keep on moving. Because of this propensity to hurl headlong into adventure, he rarely stops to think. Passion is all. The feelings of the moment are the only consideration because Ares embodies the present, the eternal now, and has no interest in the dreamy past or fictional future.

The Birth of Ares

As Zeus and Hera were Ares' parents, it was expected that he would be favoured by them. Zeus had many children by different lovers, and Hera had cast Hephaestus from Olympus because he was not the image of the 'perfect' god, so it would be only natural for Ares to be schooled as the next in line for the Olympian throne. But his quixotic parents could not bring themselves to forge a bond with him, and Ares entered a world that seemed devoid of tenderness. This was amplified by his early experiences, as he was locked within a bronze jar for a long period by two antagonists and left for dead.

Hermes eventually came to the rescue and released Ares, who was then sent to be tutored by Hermes' son, Priapus, who was a skilled dancer and so physically well-endowed that a fertility cult arose in his name. Ares was taught the art of dance before developing his skills as a warrior.

Personality Traits

Ares was impetuous, hot-tempered and quick to notice slights, with a thirst for battle and bloodshed and an innate need to prove himself. He was scorned by his family, apart from Aphrodite, who loved him and bore him three children. Their two sons, Deimos and Phobos, rode into battle with him and fought beside him, inspiring fear and panic wherever they went.

Ares was a loyal and protective father, sensitive to the rejection he had suffered at the hands of his parents and determined to come to the aid of his offspring whenever they needed him. The rules of the gods meant nothing to him if a child was in danger, and he ensured that the death in battle of his son Ascalaphus was swiftly avenged. Ares had numerous children by many women. Among these, in his Roman incarnation as Mars, he fathered Romulus and Remus, twin boys who were suckled by a wolf and grew up to become the founders of Rome.

The Romans worshipped and respected Mars, who embodied many attributes that were considered praiseworthy. To the Greeks, Ares was too uncontrollable, too ready to engage in violence, too unpredictable with his passions and frenzies. The Romans viewed Mars as the second-most important god after Jupiter (Zeus) and built temples in which to worship him. He was tall and strong, exuding masculinity and was usually depicted with a breastplate, shield and helmet. Mars was the patron of Rome through his paternity to Romulus and Remus and as the protector and benefactor of Rome's citizens.

His reputation as a natural dancer, fierce warrior and passionate lover made him a favourite with women and a strong ally to the men whom he favoured. His support of the underdog was apparent through his intense involvement in the Trojan War. This was set in motion by Aphrodite. Paris was one of the sons of King Priam of Troy and was asked to settle an argument between Aphrodite, Athena and Hera about who was the most beautiful. Each goddess promised him gifts in return for the prize of a golden apple, and Paris succumbed to Aphrodite's offer of the fairest woman in the world, who was Helen, wife of King Menelaus, and won her as his prize. Helen fell in love with Paris and gladly agreed to elope with him to Troy, but the gods became involved when Menelaus declared war. Ares, with his sons Deimos and Phobos, rushed to the aid of the Trojans, which did not endear him to the Greeks.

Warrior and Dancer

The combinations of dance and war may appear incompatible, but both involve a necessity to connect with the passions, a trait that Ares possessed to the fullest. He was intensely physical, governed by a constant urge to action, and the intricate steps of dance could be utilised on the battlefield. A successful warrior who aims to survive has to gauge in advance the moves of his opponent and take steps that enable him to avoid injury while engaging in the thrust and parry of a dance between life and death. Intuition, skill and courage carry equal value in dance and battle, and a fearless attitude is essential. Ares was no strategist; he lacked cool logic and the ability to distance himself emotionally and so was influenced by immediacy rather than long-term plans. But his loyalty to those whom he felt a bond with was absolute.

Ares' protectiveness made him a fearsome enemy. When his daughter Alcippe was raped by a son of the god of the sea, Poseidon, Ares killed him instantly. He followed his instincts, which often led him into trouble, but was usually on the side of those who were oppressed.

Relationships

Unusually among the gods, Ares, though taking many lovers, had long-lived affairs that often produced several children with one woman. He had a reputation as a great lover because of his passionate nature, his impetuosity, his spontaneity and, like Aphrodite, his ability to focus fully on the person in his arms at that moment.

His most celebrated love affair was with Aphrodite, who bore him three children. In Roman myths, their fourth child was Eros (as Cupid). They were each loyal to the other in their own way, and Aphrodite more than once interceded on Ares' behalf to the extent of physically dragging him out of harm's way. But Ares could be jealous. When Aphrodite was enamoured of the handsome mortal Adonis, Ares turned himself into a fierce wild boar and killed him with his tusks. Even so, Aphrodite returned to him again and again.

Ares' children, especially those with Aphrodite, carried the qualities of both parents. Their sons Deimos and Phobos inherited the wildest aspects of Ares and rejoiced in the blood and mayhem of the battlefield. Their daughter Harmonia carried the highest qualities of both parents and was the goddess of harmony. She married Cadmus, who had offended Ares by slaying a sacred snake and, as punishment, was made to serve Ares until he was forgiven. Cadmus, the son of the king of Phoenicia, founded the city of Thebes and brought the Phoenician alphabet to Greece.

Sibling Rivalry

Ares was the least popular of the Greek gods. His impatient, impetuous nature and bloodthirsty aspect antagonised most of the other deities, who valued logic and order and despised emotional upheaval and outpourings. His relationship with both parents was difficult and they neglected to stand up for him when other Olympians hurt or shunned him.

Chief among his adversaries was Athena, who took advantage of every opportunity to humiliate Ares, to the point of physically attacking him. Ares, unlike his siblings, acted in the moment and spent his temper quickly. He did not bear grudges. His fire, when provoked, burned fast and furious until it ran out of fuel and then he would calm down and carry on as though nothing had happened.

Ares' involvement in the Trojan War brought him more disfavour with several of his siblings. The gods concerned themselves with mortals only when it suited them and, although the Olympian family took sides in the war, on the whole they stayed aloof. Ares' stubborn and energetic support of the Trojans arose through his passionate belief in their cause and his frequent support of what he perceived as the underdog. This sparked many more clashes with Athena, who was on the side of Greece.

Archetypal Resonance

Ares as an archetype embodies the urge towards action and reaction. The surge of adrenaline, the need for physicality and the untrammelled pursuit of impulses is typical of the Ares archetype. The needs of the body call more urgently than the needs of the mind, and slights as well as desires must be acted on instantly. The emotions are charged and there is a sense of pleasure and excitement in indulging them, whether through heated argument, brawling, or sexual activity.

There is no subtlety in the Ares archetype and therefore none of the mind games or manipulative tendencies that are present in other archetypes. With Ares, what you see is what you get; the passions simmer on the surface, ready to burst into flame at the slightest encouragement.

This need for physical expression can be seen in those who battle against seemingly insuperable odds. Athletes, sports people, and fighters such as boxers and wrestlers all embody aspects of Ares, as they test themselves to their limits and beyond.

Ares' qualities, when placed in perspective, accord with the archetypal image of maleness: the hunter who brings home sustenance and ensures the survival of his family through keeping the territory safe; the ardent lover, the protective father. Our modern society now tends to favour the less Arian qualities in men and promotes a softer, more diluted version. Yet without the intervention of the Ares archetype, who was willing to fight for a place of safety for his loved ones, our culture may not have survived. The positive attributes of the Ares archetype are factors that allow men to connect with and experience their power in a manner that is constructive rather than destructive. The upsurge of men's movements and the popularity of authors such as Robert Bly, whose book *Iron John* acted as a clarion call for men to acknowledge their masculinity, signifies that the Ares archetype is alive and still fighting and desperate for healthy self-expression.

The Ares archetype in the female psyche is channelled through raw emotional expression, assertiveness, competitiveness and a refusal to be part of 'the system'.

The Qualities of Mars

As the fourth planet from the Sun and our closest neighbour, Mars engenders a deep fascination. Evidence suggests that it once held abundant supplies of water and possibly life, although now only small amounts of water can be seen at its polar ice caps. The orbit of

Mars is more elliptical (or more eccentric) than most, reflecting the unpredictable temperament of the god, and this is partly due to extraordinary surface temperature variations, which shift between −133 and +27 degrees Celsius. Although smaller than Earth, Mars has a similar-sized land-surface area because of its lack of water. Its colour has brought it the title of 'The Red Planet', and its satellites, Deimos and Phobos, are named after Ares' sons.

The qualities of the planet hold resonances with the god in both his Greek and Roman incarnations. The Roman Mars was an agriculturist before becoming a warrior and there has been a long-term fascination with the possibility of life on Mars and whether communities could be set up on the planet. The colour of Mars reflects Ares' propensity to 'see red' and to charge into the fray without forethought.

In Your Natal Chart

The position of Mars in your natal chart reveals your desires and your mode of action. The qualities of action, aggression, determination, ambition, sexuality, impulsiveness and competitiveness are expressed through the lenses of the sign and house that Mars is found in. Levels of energy, robustness and the ability to take the initiative stem from the Mars position, and aspects to other planets show how these qualities are expressed and utilised.

The aspects of Mars reflect the use of your energy and drive. Positive aspects enhance the attributes of courage, forcefulness, protectiveness, independence, leadership and strength. Negative aspects bring to light tendencies towards selfishness and self-centredness, overt aggression, violence and abuse, and indicate how those traits are likely to manifest.

Freedom to act is vital to Mars. Too many constraints create intense frustration that leads to fury and destructiveness. Yet too few constraints from other planets in the natal chart can also have a detrimental effect, as Mars needs gentle boundaries that give a sense of safety and help to defuse the more challenging characteristics.

In a man's chart, Mars reflects how he feels about his maleness and how he expresses this. In a woman's chart, Mars often indicates through sign and house what type of man she is likely to be attracted to, as well as how she expresses her personal energy and drive, and in which areas of life she is most likely to be assertive.

Rulership of Mars

Mars rules the astrological sign Aries and is co-ruler of Scorpio, having been assigned rulership of that sign before Pluto was discovered. The ram, symbol of Aries, illustrates the headstrong qualities of the astrological sign, whereas the scorpion reveals the fierce refusal to back down when challenged.

The Arian psyche is direct, with tremendous energy, drive and enthusiasm that make life an exciting experience. There is a love of the new and untried, because this accentuates the joyful challenge of pitting the wits against the unknown. As with Ares, whose rejection by his family led him to constantly attempt to prove himself, people born under the sign of Aries are eager and impatient to make their mark on the world. Aries must be first, and yearns to be recognised and admired by others, and this makes for a propensity to take risks in order to achieve goals.

An element that is lacking in this sign is staying power. Action must bear swift results, or Arians lose interest and move on. But the energy that is generated when things are going well can act as fuel that inspires others and breaks new ground.

The Arian impulsiveness and tendency to argue while not wishing to listen to the ideas, opinions, or explanations of others can make them frustrating opponents. Aries dislikes being pinned down, can be opinionated and is a reluctant listener, always in a hurry to make life happen and accomplish the task in hand. When others insist on lengthy consideration, Arians become frustrated and antagonistic, resorting to the use of verbal or physical force if they feel that is the only solution.

Defeat is anathema to Ares and to Arians. Their ability to keep going against apparently insurmountable odds makes them able to achieve a great deal. They are competitive and make strong leaders because of their courage and because they are happiest and most loyal to their supporters when they are in a position of power.

The Ares archetype when expressed through its rulership of Scorpio is a figure to be reckoned with. The emotional intensity of this combination can be a powerful force for good or ill. There are tremendous inner resources and a staying power that is lacking in the Aries counterpart. This can lead to risk-taking and a willingness to engage in death-defying acts in order to accomplish goals. There are no half-measures and this can bring about extraordinary achievements or appalling degradation.

Situations such as Ares' slaying of Aphrodite's lover Adonis are a dire illustration of the Scorpio connection with Ares, as the passions are so intense and inflammatory that jealousy and possessiveness can be a challenging issue. Yet this combination of archetype and sign can make them, though uncompromising, loyal to the point of giving all for those to whom they are affiliated.

CHAPTER SEVEN

Jupiter ♃
Zeus

The archetype of the king, the leader, defines the essential qualities of Zeus. As father and ruler of the Olympians, his task is to control his unruly family and to ensure that the dynasty remains powerful.

Zeus embodies the urge to create harmony in the environment through facilitating growth both internally and externally. His many lovers and children were an extension of his need to be assured of the perpetuity of the clan. His intelligence gives him the ability to see far beyond the range of other gods and mortals. His focus is outward, on the wider vision and the future.

The Birth of Zeus

Zeus was the youngest of six children born to Rhea and Cronus, her brother and consort. Cronus had come to power through overthrowing his father, Uranus, but when Rhea became pregnant he heeded a prophecy that dictated his loss of power at the hands of a son. Determined not to allow this, he swallowed each of his first five children at birth.

During her pregnancy with Zeus, Rhea begged her parents to help her, and on their advice tricked Cronus with a stone wrapped in swaddling clothes when Zeus was born. Her youngest child grew up in safety and sought help from Metis, goddess of wisdom, who allied him with the Titans in order to defeat his father. Metis gave Zeus a potion made from powerful emetic herbs that he forced down the gullet of his father, so that Cronus would vomit up the children that he had swallowed. The five older siblings were Hades, Poseidon, Hestia, Demeter and Hera, and the three brothers divided the realms between them through drawing lots. Hades won the underworld as his realm, Poseidon took the sea, and Zeus became ruler of the heavens and Mount Olympus.

Personality Traits

Zeus, in effect, became lord of the Earth as well as the heavens. To the best of his ability, he was a just and fair ruler. He favoured logic and reason, set laws that both gods and mortals were well advised to follow, and so began the age of the Olympian gods. As deity of thunder and lightning, his retribution was fierce and swift if he was displeased, but as god of rain he vivified the earth and all living things.

As a ruler, Zeus embodied power and enjoyed exerting his authority. He attained his position through a combination of force and his ability to inspire others and earn their goodwill and co-operation. His totem, the eagle, represented his ability to take a bird's-eye view, to look down from above and see the totality rather than merely details.

Zeus was a natural leader and mediator and was frequently called upon to intercede in the affairs of members of his family. When Apollo complained to him that Hermes had stolen his cattle, Zeus insisted that Hermes hand over his newly made lyre in exchange. He cared deeply for most of his children and birthed two of them from his own body. He carried his son Dionysus stitched into his thigh until the child was ready to be born, after Semele, Dionysus' mortal mother died during the pregnancy. He birthed Athena from his forehead and furnished Artemis with her bow and arrows and her band of nymphs. He could be generous and kind, yet there was also a crueller aspect to his nature.

There are two versions of the story of the birth of Hephaestus. In one, recounted in Chapter 5, Hephaestus was cast from Olympus by his mother, Hera, because he was born with a club foot. Another tale describes how Zeus, angry that Hephaestus took Hera's side during an argument, threw his son to Earth, leaving him permanently crippled. Zeus despised his son Ares and consistently denied him any affection.

Zeus was an expert at gathering support around him. When he overthrew his father, Cronus, he was helped by the Titans, and rewarded them by re-establishing the freedom that Cronus had taken from them. His keen sense of justice enabled him to find ways in which to mediate in arguments and disputes between the immortals, and he kept the peace as effectively as was possible in what would in modern terms be viewed as a rowdy and dysfunctional family. In so doing, he earned their respect.

The urge for procreation was strong in Zeus and is a characteristic of his archetypal nature as king of the gods. Producing progeny is necessary for a ruler whose goal is to found a new dynasty, and Zeus had many children, most of them illegitimate.

Sky God

As god of the sky, Zeus could watch over the Earth and observe the ways of men as well as gods. He invested earthly kings with their power and created and enforced the laws that others had to follow. His justice and retribution were swift, indisputable and final, and any who crossed him were punished, but his generous, mostly benevolent nature preferred harmony to reign.

The realm of the sky and the air denotes intellectual qualities, and Zeus favoured logic and reason above all else. His dislike of Ares stemmed from his son's impetuousness and what Zeus considered a lack of forethought and common sense. The two realms of the mind, logical and abstract, were the domain of Zeus and this overruled the feeling nature. Excessive displays of emotion made him impatient and angry, but he could be appealed to through reason.

The nature of Zeus was expansive. This was reflected in his family through his numerous offspring; in his lordship over the boundless heavens and through his position on the throne of Olympus; and within his mind, through the vast spaces that he occupied, and ruled with a philosophical attitude.

Relationships

Before and after his marriage to Hera, Zeus had numerous liaisons with nymphs, Titans and mortal women. Many of them bore him children. Before Hera, Zeus was romantically linked with Metis, Themis, Eurynome, Demeter, Mnemosyne and Leto – the kin of his parents. He attempted to seduce Hera through playing on her sympathies as a small, helpless bird, but she refused to become his lover and persuaded him to marry her.

Zeus' affairs were legendary, as was Hera's fury and jealousy, which impelled her to punish his lovers and their children rather than her errant husband. Although many stories are told of Hera as the wronged and angry wife, their union was happy most of the time and Zeus always returned to her after he had strayed.

Many of the gods were children of Zeus. Among them were Hermes, through Zeus' affair with Maia; Dionysus, god of wine and ecstasy; Ares, Hephaestus, Artemis and Apollo, and the nine Muses through Mnemosyne (Memory). Apart from Ares and Hephaestus, he maintained a positive relationship with his children.

Zeus also had at least one male lover. He abducted Ganymede, a handsome young man from Troy, and made him his cup-bearer. Zeus immortalised the youth as the constellation Aquarius, the Water-bearer, and one of the moons of Jupiter is named after him.

Sibling Rivalry

Zeus was the rescuer of his brothers and sisters, and the domains of sky, sea and underworld were divided between Zeus, Poseidon and Hades, who, with their sisters, became the first Olympians and their consorts.

Relationships were generally positive, but Zeus offended Demeter, goddess of the earth and motherhood, when their daughter Persephone was abducted by Hades, and Zeus ignored Persephone's cries for help. His excuse was that he had no wish to interfere with the affairs of his brother, even at the risk of losing his daughter.

Zeus and Hera, brother and sister as well as consorts, held equal power. Despite Zeus' philandering and Hera's outrage over it, they remained married and true to their chosen roles.

Archetypal Resonance

Zeus as an archetype embodies the role of king of the psyche; the wise, all-seeing leader who can gain the trust of others and inspire them to carry out his bidding. He was master of all he surveyed, capable, authoritarian, certain of his power and able to keep it because those around him respected him.

As creator and upholder of laws, Zeus dispensed judgements and justice and was a fair mediator through his ability as sky god to see a situation in its entirety and come to a workable solution. His word was law, and woe betide any who ignored Zeus, as he would strike them down instantly.

The Zeus archetype manifests as a driving will that is aimed at gathering and consolidating power. When all is going well, peace, harmony and benevolence reign. But in conflict, the power is held on to or retrieved at any cost and the adversary is made to pay dearly.

A love of women is also prominent in the Zeus archetype, rather as in the case of a male animal surrounded by a selection of females that can blend new mixtures in the gene pool and assure the continuity of the species. Women are seen to have their place as lovers and consorts, but less frequently as friends, as the Zeus archetype is a ladies' man for the pleasure he gains through the sexual act and through the result of future progeny. In some of his affairs, Zeus assumed other forms. He came to Danae, mother of the hero Perseus, and impregnated her in the form of a golden shower. Europa was seduced by him in the guise of a white bull, and Leda by a swan. This implies that the joy of the conquest and impregnation were paramount.

The Zeus archetype is not domesticated and is certainly not willing to damage his mantle by taking on what he would consider as women's work. The role is that of head of the family and of the wider family of the realm he governs.

The Qualities of Jupiter

This immense gas giant, larger than all of the planets in the solar system put together, lies beyond the asteroid belt and is aptly named Jupiter, after the Roman incarnation of the sky god. Jupiter has many moons, with the largest, Io, Ganymede, Europa and Callisto, named after lovers of Zeus. The bands of colour that are visible around the planet are caused by winds as they blow in opposite directions. Storms rage on Jupiter, bringing turbulent clouds of gas that fill the atmosphere with ammonia. The nature of the Jovian atmosphere reflects Zeus' rulership as god of thunder and lightning.

The surface of Jupiter is neither earthy nor rocky. The atmosphere of ammonia clouds filters down to a layer of frozen gases and then deeper, to a mantle of hydrogen. The planet radiates about four times as much heat as it receives from the Sun, which suggests that it possesses an internal source of heat and fuel. Recent scientific discoveries have linked the orbit of Jupiter to sunspot cycles. Sunspots peak just after Jupiter passes perihelion, the phase when Jupiter is moving at its fastest, when it is changing direction and the planet's gravitational force is at its most powerful. This connection between Zeus and Apollo, the Sun god and most favoured son, affects us on Earth, as sunspots are linked, among other things, to weather systems on our planet.

Around fifty light years from our solar system, a star named Beta Pictoris displays evidence of its own planetary system. Within it is a planet estimated to be similar in size and characteristics to Jupiter, which resonates with Zeus' control over other domains far from Olympus.

Zeus' qualities as the most prominent god, whose generative abilities were second to none, are easily understood in the context of the planet that bears his Roman name. The nature of Jupiter, with its physical attributes as lord of the planets, corresponds closely with the position of the god in the Greek pantheon.

In Your Natal Chart

Jupiter's position in your natal chart reveals information about your ethical, philosophical and spiritual (especially religious) codes and beliefs. The qualities of benevolence, growth, expansion, generosity, intelligence and goodwill stem from the sign and house that Jupiter is found in. Material benefits and the respect of others are indicated, according to whether the planet is positively or negatively aspected by others, along with your ability to make the most of 'good luck'.

The word 'jovial' has a strong resonance with this planet, because generally the characteristic of Jupiter energy is bonhomie. As the largest planet and the archetypal ruler of the sky, the expansive nature of Jupiter embodies an urge for success and recognition and a desire to ensure that all is well with the world.

As a deity, Zeus did not seek conflict and he was a skilful mediator when problems were laid at his feet. The demeanour of the god was of one who much preferred to watch over his domains with an all-seeing eye, while he enjoyed the company of those who pleased him. He took his role seriously and allowed Hera equal status in a distinctly patriarchal regime. He respected Athena's warlike aspect and admired her intelligence.

Jupiter embodies power that is earned and then accepted naturally, as a matter of course. Co-operation is viewed as a necessary quality that makes life more comfortable for all, and the wider view is always taken into account. Decisions that are made attempt to take all sides of the situation into account − but once made, are final.

The house that Jupiter rests in shows the area in which the Jovian qualities are experienced and expressed, and reflects where positive action is most likely to be channelled.

When well aspected, Jupiter expresses expansion, optimism, generosity, solid inner faith and good fortune; and ensures that you will be in the right place at the right time to receive the many-tiered benefits of its planetary influence. Negative aspects can reveal either an authoritarian attitude that seeks always to be right and cannot admit mistakes, or an over-expansiveness that can lead to financial problems or unwanted excessive weight gain.

Jupiter, like Zeus, enjoys the good things of life, and the areas of the natal chart where this planet is found are infused with energy, enthusiasm and a positive attitude.

Rulership of Jupiter

Jupiter rules the astrological sign Sagittarius; the Centaur with his bow and arrow, who can move fast and aim true. The Jovian psyche is honest and open, direct in speech and truthful to the point of giving offence, as there is little subtlety and much need to give voice to thoughts. A love of freedom, a tremendous pleasure in play and the company of animals as well as people, and a natural inclination towards leadership make this archetype difficult to put in a box. Whichever mindset Jupiter encompasses is likely to be continually outgrown because of the inherent need for expansion.

The capacity for deep thought and a concern for the well-being of others makes the Jovian archetype a fair and generous leader. A conventional aspect, a need to know that certain rules and regulations are there for the benefit of all, can manifest as rigidity or bigotry if Jupiter is badly aspected. But generally there is an interest in discussion, a love of roaming the terrain of the mind, especially in the area of abstract thought; the deeper and more profound this is, the more it is welcomed and enjoyed.

A craving for adventure brings a constant search for new horizons, intellectually and physically. Zeus' many affairs were a reflection of his need for romantic adventures and his resistance to being kept too closely by the side of his loyal wife. The Jovian psyche tends to fulfil these needs by embarking on adventures of the mind, or through travelling and exploring the world.

The Zeus personality is innately positive and forward-oriented. Energy is high, often exuberant, and needs to be channelled. A goal to move towards is important, particularly if the attainment of that goal brings respect and acclaim from others. A natural urge to like and be liked can be overruled by the need to be right.

Love of a traditional, workable system stems from Zeus' reign over Olympus. The place of each archetypal figure was assured and tended to remain true to type. The need for a system contributed to a code for measuring and assuring good conduct and as harmonious a way of life as possible.

Jupiter co-rules Pisces, alongside Neptune. The expansive aspects of the planet and archetype are expressed here through the qualities of love and compassion and a benevolent attitude. A tendency to take care of others and to take their needs or demands to heart can lead to a willingness to accept more responsibility than is healthy, as this does not create the space for allowing responsibility and autonomy in the person who is being helped. Zeus was willing to intercede in disputes in order to avoid further conflict — but some of the quarrels between the deities could have been effectively resolved between themselves. In this role Zeus, as with the Jupiter–Pisces connection, takes on the role of father of all, whose authority, wisdom and beneficent nature are sometimes taken advantage of.

Wherever Jupiter is found in the natal chart indicates the willingness and ability to grow. The existence within the psyche of the tremendous potential for positive expression of the will encourages other internal voices to speak with more harmony.

CHAPTER EIGHT

Saturn ♄
Cronus

The laws of karma, of cause and effect, are attributed to Cronus. As god of time he reminds us that all things must pass, and that we must learn to take responsibility for our actions in order to avoid repeating the mistakes of the past.

Cronus embodies the cycles of action and reaction that ultimately lead to change and growth. The method he employs is that of restriction, of understanding the nature of limitation in order to transcend this. His ways are often harsh, but eventually lead to a greater degree of self-knowledge. The essential nature of Cronus is that of the stern teacher who has no use for fripperies or embellishments. Yet if we pay attention to his advice, another aspect emerges: the rich harvest of crops that are gained through ploughing and weeding the fields of the self.

The Birth of Cronus

Cronus was the youngest son of Gaia, the Earth goddess, and Uranus, the sky god. So fertile was Gaia that Uranus became jealous, and imprisoned her children by sealing them deep within her body.

When Cronus was born, Gaia hid him from his father and waited for him to grow strong. She then armed him with a sickle of grey stone to use as a weapon. Leaping out of hiding during the sexual act, Cronus severed the genitals of his father and cast them into the sea. Aphrodite rose from the waves, and the Erinyes from the droplets of blood that flew through the air. The fierce reign of Uranus came to an end and Cronus released his mother from the burden of his siblings and took the throne.

Personality Traits

There are chilling similarities between the births of Cronus and that of his own son, Zeus. Both were sons who, in order to gain their lives and their power as leaders, rebelled against and destroyed their fathers. The need to survive against all odds engendered drastic measures, and Zeus allied himself with his father's siblings in order to crush the harsh rule of his father, deploying their natural primal energy in his favour.

Cronus, however, once he had defeated Uranus, was determined to rule alone. He chained up his brothers and sisters, the Titans, thereby creating the resentment that would lead them to later join with his son against him when he attempted to deny life to his own offspring.

As new ruler of the gods, Cronus took his authority seriously. He married his sister Rhea, an earth goddess cast in the mould of her mother and who, like Gaia, suffered when her husband grew resentful of her and fearful of losing his hard-won place as primary god. The first generation of Olympians were born, but only survived through Rhea's determination to hide her youngest son, in the hope that, like his father before him, he would overthrow her husband and rescue his siblings.

Cronus was stern and unbending. He intended to keep to himself the power that he had gathered, and he grasped that power jealously. Instead of sharing rulership with his siblings, the Titans, he imprisoned them, restricting the forces of nature that they embodied. He was a hard taskmaster, rigid in his approach, determined to set and maintain a status quo, allowing nothing to interfere with his autonomy.

God of Time

Cronus was the god of time, who sets the laws and yet is beyond them. The word 'chronology' belongs to him. 'Chronic', implying a continuing condition that persists over time, derives from his name, as does 'chronicle', a story that is written in order of events. His rule was long, and even when his role as king of the gods came to an end, Cronus himself survived, and entered his next incarnation in a more beneficent form as the Roman god Saturn.

As Saturn he was viewed very positively by the Romans. It seems that he mellowed and took on new qualities. To them he was Father Time, the ruler of a golden age where death and disease did not exist. In ancient Roman tales, Saturn, after his defeat at the hands of Jupiter (Zeus), made Italy his home, and was highly revered.

Just as Cronus / Saturn swallowed his children, so also does time swallow mortal lives, and is noticed only through its passing, and continues through future generations.

Saturnalia

This festival in honour of Saturn in his role as the god of agriculture was held initially on the 17th December and later was extended to encompass the days between the 17th and 23rd December. In modern times we call this festival Yule, but its original title, Saturnalia, still continues in the pagan tradition.

In contrast to the dour image of a dark and vengeful god held by the Greeks, Saturn had a 'work hard and play hard' reputation with the Romans. Saturnalia was the most popular festival of the year, and occurred at the time when Roman farmers had finished their autumn planting.

It began with a ritual during which sacrifices were made to the god. A statue depicting him with bonds around his feet and carrying a sickle was made the central focus of the ceremony. The bonds were loosened, to symbolically liberate him anew each year, and this was followed by feasting, with an image of the god present at the banquet so that he could join the feast and subsequent merriment. Gifts of wax candles were exchanged, symbolising the lengthening days and the return of the light. Slaves were given their freedom for the duration of the festival, and were waited on by their masters. Laws were relaxed and criminals pardoned. Dress was casual rather than formal, and public gambling was permitted. An atmosphere of jollity, equality and informality reigned, often to the extent of open debauchery.

Doors, windows and the people themselves were garlanded with greenery; particularly holly, as Saturn was viewed as the holly king, while Jupiter was the oak king. Gilded cakes were made and eaten, shaped as moons, stars and animals, to encourage fertility over the coming year. This was a popular time for conception.

Relationships

The Greek portrayal of Cronus was not loveable. Slayer of his infanticidal father, who then absorbed the same pattern and was in turn disempowered by his son, Cronus' ability to bond was poor. As a husband he wanted the sole attention of his wife, and this alienated her and brought her to betray him in order to give life to her children, as her mother had done before her with her husband. As a brother he bound his siblings and kept them from experiencing the freedom that their father had also denied them. Ultimately, his constricted rule cost him dearly in the Greek version of his myths.

His procreative powers were great, and brought about a new dynasty that, try as he might, he could not prevent from coming into being. He was held back from any pride or pleasure in paternity by the fear that his progeny would take what was his. Cronus was unwilling to share, and, in the myths of the Ancient Greeks, he paid the price by losing all that he valued.

In his Roman incarnation, however, the loss of his domain led to something more beneficial to all, and particularly to mortals. The Golden Age that Saturn heralded was a time of peace and plenty when restrictions were lifted, and the breaking of rules and laws was forgiven rather than punished at his honoured time. Sharing took the place of withholding, and the god finally found a place for himself in the light – revered, respected and loved.

Sibling Rivalry

Cronus could have invented the term 'sibling rivalry'. He freed the Titans from the belly of Gaia, their mother, only to imprison them once more to prevent them from holding any power that he considered to be rightfully his. In part this was a punishment against them because when Gaia pleaded for help, only Cronus was willing and able to come to her aid. This was not the fault of his siblings, forced as they were to endure the darkness of the earth's depths, but Cronus had a resentful aspect, and had no intention of dividing his realm for those beings who had inadvertently caused pain to his mother.

Yet their influence persisted through unions with his own progeny. Mnemosyne, goddess of memory, birthed the Muses, the forces who inspire the heights of art and creativity, through her affair with Zeus, the son of Cronus. Themis, Titan goddess of justice and order, also entered into a relationship with Zeus before he married Hera, and so did Demeter, another earth goddess, like her mother. Several of the sisters of Cronus had children by the son who overthrew him, and those unions populated the worlds of gods and mortals with beings who added shape and texture to the Olympian myths. Ultimately, the god of time saw his family expand to the horizons that he had attempted to deprive them of.

Archetypal Resonance

Cronus as an archetype embodies the stern father who is incapable of feeling or receiving affection because he never received love from his own father. More recently, we see this in the repressed attitudes of the Victorian era, in which the father was expected to be an authority figure, all-powerful, whose word is law and who must be obeyed for fear of harsh retribution.

As the son who must find his own power and display it in order to gain a place in the world, the Cronus archetype has the ambition, the tenacity and the planning power to carry out his self-assigned tasks. But once this power is gained, constriction occurs. What is held on to no longer brings pleasure, because the fear of losing what you have gained is greater than the joy of ownership. In this aspect, Cronus is similar to the miser who locks away what is most beautiful and valuable to him in order to prevent others from coveting it.

There are positive qualities, however. These are self-discipline, the ability to set a goal and then reach it, surmounting all obstacles that stand in the way. There is tremendous patience and endurance and the knowledge that time is a commodity and can be utilised. The Golden Age of Saturn made boundaries appreciated because they created safety and stability. When restrictions were temporarily abandoned at Saturnalia, the sense of equality and freedom created a widespread state of euphoria.

In his Roman guise, this archetype provides a flip-side to the Cronus / Saturn coin. As father of the gods, and as procreator and fertility symbol, he represents hard work that is rewarded by the fruits of labour, and embodies an undercurrent of sexuality and rampant life-force that, though suppressed for much of the time, cannot be permanently suppressed. Once the work has been done, the play can begin.

The Qualities of Saturn

A gas giant, like Jupiter, Uranus and Neptune, and the second-largest planet in our solar system, Saturn has a similar composition to Jupiter. The planet is 95 times heavier than Earth and its light takes just over an hour to reach us. The winds at Saturn's equator are the fastest in the solar system, averaging 1,200 miles (1,900 kilometres) per hour.

Saturn's rings are composed of billions of small chunks of ice, and are an intriguing feature of the planet. Jupiter and Neptune both have a faint nimbus created by surrounding debris, but the rings of Saturn are so prominent and dense that they cannot be missed. These tiny ice chunks are thought to have come from the formation of a moon that was too close to Saturn's gravitational pull to survive intact, and broke up into countless pieces that are trapped in orbit around the planet. These rings add to Saturn's beauty, and also illustrate the symbolic resonance of the god, who in his Greek form represents restriction, boundaries and limitation. The planet is, in a sense, the prisoner of its satellites, contained within their eternal dance while he, in the centre, moves alone.

In Your Natal Chart

The position of Saturn in your natal chart reveals the areas in which you become aware of responsibilities, restrictions and limitations. Your obligations, your career and your responses to discipline and hard work are all indicated by Saturn. This planet is concerned with stability, security and a sense of order, and gives clues as to which aspects of your life are taken seriously. It also shows your attitudes towards authority and father-figures.

Status and recognition are Saturnian concerns, and accomplishment is highly valued. Short-term benefits are of lesser importance than achievements that can be seen to have long-term effects.

Saturn is concerned with boundaries. When it is positively aspected, these provide a safe container within which to work and, once those boundaries have been outgrown, new ones are set that allow for further growth and development. Saturn is a teacher, who advocates self-discipline and effort in order to attain goals one step at a time. Where other planetary influences can give an urge to run before you can walk, Saturn is cautious, setting rules and guidelines, plodding steadily on up the highest mountain that can be found. That determination brings you to the summit, though this may take time, patience and tenacity.

Willpower is strong wherever this planet is placed in the natal chart. It bestows an ability to concentrate; to define, set and accomplish tasks. When aspects to Saturn are difficult, there can be tendencies to depression and low self-esteem and either an inability to be disciplined, or attitudes that are so repressed, tight and restricted that they hinder growth and vitality.

Every 29 years, Saturn completes its cycle around the Sun and returns to its original position in the natal chart. During this period, known as Saturn's Return, which occurs around ages 29, 58 and 87, issues that have not been previously dealt with come to the fore. This time is sometimes naively viewed negatively, and reputed to be difficult and unhappy — mainly because important life-changes such as relationship break-ups or loss of a job can occur during this influence. Often there is an urge to clear the past, and to settle down, so some feel a sudden urge to start a family. In essence, Saturn's Return brings the planet's teaching qualities to the fore, and if this is appreciated and worked with it can be immensely useful. In this respect, Saturn can be viewed as the rather stern taskmaster who can slap your wrist if you have not been paying attention to developing your potential, but who then provides opportunities for sloppy habits to be overcome, and so facilitates growth, empowerment and maturity.

Through its Greek aspect, the planet Saturn embodies the need to overcome small-mindedness and pettiness, to create safe boundaries and to be aware of limitations while simultaneously understanding that too much rigidity is unhealthy and counter-productive. Through its Roman aspect, the planet acts as a reminder that necessary work leads to accomplishment and bears its own rewards. A strong Saturn can act as a framework that holds the other planetary influences in place, and allows the maximum fulfilment of potential.

Rulership of Saturn

Saturn rules the astrological sign Capricorn, represented by the symbol of a sturdy, sure-footed goat that is determined to reach the top of the mountain, the pinnacle of achievement, and is capable of surmounting any obstacles that stand in the way. The Capricornian psyche is conscientious and determined, ambitious and well organised, with a powerful inner drive that keeps them on track even when the terrain is rough.

There is a conventional bent to the Capricornian mind; a desire to be conventional, to not stand out too much in a crowd. This can initially make them appear rather solemn and constrained, even dogmatic, and if challenged they will do their utmost to come out on top. Because of their sound common sense, they think things through carefully and thoroughly before acting, and plan their route meticulously, so that every contingency is allowed for in order to minimise any risk of mistakes or failure.

Although Capricornians appear to be quiet and well behaved, they tend to subscribe to the motto 'rule from beneath', and their self-belief and tenacity makes them strive for a dominant position in both the workplace and at home. Materialistic urges stem from a craving for security, and they acquire possessions and wealth through being careful with what they have. Prudence is a key aspect of the Capricornian nature.

When young, Capricornians appear older than their years and exhibit a quiet maturity that leads them to take on responsibility willingly. But as they age, they 'grow into' themselves, and after maturity often appear youthful in both looks and attitude.

The Cronus aspect of Saturn manifests as stinginess and small-mindedness, and in grasping for more in order to hold on to security. Fear of lack acts as a driving force for achievement. The Saturn aspect manifests as a hard worker with a dry, wry sense of humour, and an underlying mischievousness that can be surprising and delightful when the surface poise is penetrated.

CHAPTER NINE

Uranus

Uranus

The first father of the gods and the most unpredictable, Uranus embodies the raw power of the elements. With thunder and lightning as his tools and weapons, he impregnated the earth, Gaia, and sired the immortals, only to attempt to force them back to their source. The lightning strike of Uranus manifests as the flash of inspiration and innovation, or as the touch of death that burns the receiver into carbon, to return to the earth, who nurtured them.

The driving force of Uranus is change; from the elemental into solid form, from electricity into matter that strives to contain the uncontainable. Through exploring his domain we seek to understand that which cannot be grasped; the primal generation of pure energy in thought and form.

The Birth of Uranus

Gaia, the mother of Uranus, was the matrix from whom the gods of the future came. She herself was created through the emergence of Eros, god of love, who sprang from the void of Chaos and brought a new order of life to the universe.

The earth became the central focus for generative and procreative energy. Gaia birthed the mountains and sea and then Uranus, the sky, whom she took as her consort. Heaven and Earth came together and mated and the first gods, the Titans, came into being.

But the fear of the father – that he would be diminished by his wife's fertility and supplanted by one of his children – led to his ultimately self-destructive act of burying them within her and not allowing them to come to full birth. Gaia, shocked, sorrowful and in great pain, plotted against him to take his power and called on her children for help. Of them all, only Cronus was willing to come to her aid, and Uranus was castrated and overthrown by his son. The outcome that he feared came about.

Personality Traits

Uranus tends to receive very negative press through some of the myths, with their focus on him as a jealous husband and cruel, murderous father. But there is more to him than initially meets the eye.

As the first sky god, he was an elemental force, whose source of grounding came through Gaia, his mother and wife. Born so closely related to the void of Chaos, he inherited much of that raw, primeval, chaotic energy and was by his very nature uncontrollable and unpredictable. With Gaia, he brought the worlds into being, impregnating her with thunderbolts and lightning. The rain that issued from him fell to the earth, awakening and fertilising it, but his distaste for the children that resulted from their marriage, and his envy of Gaia's love for them, made him push them back into the earth from which they came, imprisoning them in the body of their mother.

This first generation of immortals were not what Uranus expected. The intensity of the attraction between Heaven and Earth was such that the still-chaotic creative energy that issued through him, with all its limitless potential for forms of expression, spawned an unruly and rebellious brood. This included the Titans, the Hecatoncheires – a trio of giants with a hundred hands apiece – and three Cyclopes: huge creatures with a single eye in the centre of their foreheads. Uranus, unable to control his offspring, took desperate measures and sent them back to their source, one by one. When Gaia appealed to her children for help and Cronus sprang to her aid and emasculated his father, the blood from his severed genitals fertilised the earth with his power for one final time. From this act of violence issued, among others, the Furies, who unleashed violence, hatred and anger into the world. To counterbalance this came Aphrodite, goddess of love and beauty.

Uranus has a dire reputation until you look more closely at his story. The power-hungry, vicious deity becomes one who is in a difficult position. As the father of the gods, he wanted to be proud of his children. As father to an anarchic tribe who squabbled and warred in his presence, and who challenged him to the limits of his endurance, he felt that he had no choice but to dispose of them. In doing this he earned the enmity and betrayal of the consort he loved.

His defeat at the hands of Cronus did not kill him; it merely rendered him incapable of procreation. He was reconciled with Gaia and remained her consort, even stepping in to give advice to his daughter Rhea when she begged for help in stopping Cronus from swallowing her children at birth. The god who had attempted to deprive his children of a future was now willing to help his daughter to protect her own progeny. This indicates that Uranus did not bear grudges and that the myth of the envious, patricidal god was only part of his story.

Uranus was god of the elemental forces of the storm, which are uncontrollable and unpredictable. No-one can tell where or when lightning will hit. With the Earth as his realm, he had a large enough target for strikes to take place, but Uranus lacked the boundary-setting qualities of his son Cronus, which would have given him tighter control of the elements. He later bequeathed his weapons of thunderbolts and lightning to his grandson Zeus, who used them only when necessary.

Relationships

The magnetism that repeatedly drew Uranus to Gaia was the attraction of high abstract thought that must be 'brought down to earth' in order to be effective. This ability to expand the thought processes to encompass vast spaces was a primary aspect of the god. By uniting with Gaia, the thoughts became forms and transpired to be stranger than the parents of them could possibly have imagined.

The children of Uranus rebelled against him; firstly the monsters and Titans that he and Gaia brought into being and then, when they were apparently disposed of, his youngest son, Cronus. The Uranian energy is unconventional and feels confined by boundaries, and his offspring exhibited what is now considered the typically Uranian dislike of authority. The need for space and change that Uranus so forcibly attempted to fulfil was stunted by the new restrictions that Cronus, the embodiment of the opposite of his father, imposed upon him. Yet ultimately this freed him from further physical acts of fatherhood and allowed his creative energy to be employed through the mental and imaginative facilities instead.

Siblings

The siblings of Uranus, the mountains and sea, were, like him, elemental forces. These created focal points for Uranus' self-expression. The mountains provided peaks and crannies for the god's electrical charges to travel through, resulting in changes of landscape and a playground for his power. The sea, symbol of the unconscious, provided the depth that could contain unexpressed aspects of the infinite mental energy of the sky god. Gaia's children embodied the earth, water and heavens as the unconscious, conscious and superconscious aspects of the mind.

Archetypal Resonance

Uranus as an archetype is the expression of the universal mind, in the form of flashes of insight and intuition that can be temporarily blinding and are difficult to grasp and bring down to earth. The sudden glimpses of something intangible can, if followed through, lead to an intuitive understanding of universal truths. Flashes of genius, of sudden 'knowing', are the domain of Uranus and open the doors of perception that have led to many of the most important discoveries, particularly in the sciences and spirituality, that are fundamental to our knowledge of who we are and why we are here. These perceptions are often channelled through a glimpse of the universe as various forms of energy, with patterns that are clearly, though sometimes only momentarily, seen.

The most ground-breaking scientific discoveries have begun with a lightning flash of insight and are classic expressions of the Uranian nature. The theory of gravity came about as a result of Newton pondering beneath a tree as he watched an apple fall to the ground. Einstein's famous equation $E = mc^2$ resulted from a daydream that he had about what it would be like to ride on a beam of light. The Uranian gifts most commonly reveal themselves during a receptive state of mind. There are many examples of the expression of Uranus' archetypal resonance. Yet the idea alone is not enough. It must be grounded, brought to earth, made explainable, solid and real in order to be useful – just as Uranus needed Gaia in order to express himself fully.

The energy of this archetype has wild and unpredictable qualities. It is difficult to grasp or contain, because it battles against constraints. Thought must be allowed to fly free, to soar above uncharted territory, but the seeds that drop from these excursions can be caught and planted in the earth, nourished and allowed to develop into new and wondrous forms whose shoots spread and diversify into ever widening areas.

The Qualities of Uranus

A gas giant, like its close neighbours, Jupiter and Neptune, Uranus has an atmosphere composed mostly of hydrogen with traces of methane and houses a rocky core approximately the size of Earth. Its weather changes only imperceptibly over decades, unlike that of Jupiter, which is subject to violent storms. One year on Uranus, one cycle around the Sun, is the equivalent to 84 Earth years. Yet even with its tremendous distance from the Sun (roughly 20 times that of Earth), Uranus responds to our fiery luminary by experiencing seasons. In the springtime, wisps of cloud appear in the upper atmosphere, gather, and shed their contents onto the planet — much as Uranus fertilised Gaia with storms and rain.

The planet was discovered in 1781 by William Herschel, a British astronomer, using a home-made telescope set in the garden of his house in Bath, England. Initially the planet was named after him, but its name was changed to Uranus as that name stuck, and the god's unpredictability accorded with the strange anomalies of the planet's orbit.

The orbit of Uranus is erratic and unusual because the axis is tilted and lies in the same plane as its orbit. Because of this, Uranus moves around the Sun in a motion that resembles a corkscrew, whereas other planets spin on themselves rather like a child's spinning top. It is thought that the planet was involved in a collision early in its formation that knocked a piece off it and created its extraordinary manner of travel through space. The myth of Uranus' castration by Cronus, and his subsequent withdrawal from the orbit of the Titans and Olympians, is reflected in the skies.

In Your Natal Chart

The position of Uranus in your natal chart shows how you experience and express urges towards freedom of self-expression, and your need to assert your individuality. The area of the chart in which Uranus is found reveals clues as to your soul purpose in this lifetime, especially with respect to understanding why you are here and what you can accomplish in order to find fulfilment.

This planet gives an intuitive link to the universal aspect of the mind, and the sign and house that it rests in are indicators of how that connection with the source of thought and ideas is made. The goals and aspirations that provide impetus to the defining of your sense of inner purpose (rather than the physical, material aspects ruled by Saturn) derive from the influence of Uranus. The types of friendships that you seek and feel enlivened by are also attributed to this planet, because Uranus rules group activities and situations that allow 'like minds' to connect with each other. Through this, ideas are swiftly disseminated and thought processes affect entire cultures rather than merely individuals. The Internet is a powerful illustration of Uranian energy, with its capacity to provide links and information to and between all, and its speed of accessibility.

As the planet of magnetism and the unexpected and unconventional, Uranus brings together the unusual and unlikely, and through this creates new possibilities. There is an elemental aspect to the influence of this planet. Flashes of attraction, insights, eccentricity and revelations are its domains. The urge to discover, to seek out the unknown and the unusual in order to learn, and to communicate that knowledge, are typically Uranian. Astrology, with its combination of science and insight, is ruled by Uranus.

The natal position and aspects can reveal gifts and interests in the sciences, particularly in areas such as electro-magnetism and quantum physics. The generative ability of the god that emerges through the meeting of opposites, the union of Heaven and Earth, can spawn monsters, or birth ideas that carry benefits for all.

Negative aspects can manifest as a desire to be different at any cost; as outrageous behaviour for the sake of it and as stubbornness and lack of consideration for the feelings of others.

There is a keen intelligence that underpins the Uranian energy that, coupled with humanitarian attitudes, makes for stimulating and fascinating friends whose joy in discovery touches those around them.

Rulership of Uranus

The astrological glyph for Uranus looks like an aerial set atop a circle, the symbol for the heavens connecting with the Earth. As ruler of Aquarius, the pictorial symbol is of the Water-bearer, who pours out the forces of life and spiritual energy, which vivify all that they touch. The Romans connected this astrological sign with Ganymede, the beautiful Trojan youth whom Zeus / Jupiter fell in love with and immortalised. In modern symbolism, this is represented as a female form, but the Romans considered Ganymede to have been the force to bring life-giving rain at the command of the thunder and lightning that Uranus hurled through the skies.

Aquarius carries attributes of love of humanity, independence, originality and eccentricity. As an air sign, Aquarians are thinkers. Whereas the thought processes of their fellow air signs, Gemini and Libra, are concerned with making connections with people in order to satisfy curiosity and find balance, those of Aquarius are focused on discovering and communicating higher truths that will benefit humanity across a broad scale.

The extraordinary characteristics of the god Uranus are generated through a love of the new and unusual and the quest for a higher expression of truth. Uranus brought into being a tribe of strange creatures that populated the Earth and could not be oppressed or suppressed, despite his efforts. He was the first father, the creator of forms that emerged through his connection with a greater and more complex source than his mother and consort. When there is a link with the creatrix of all possibilities, as with Uranus and Chaos, the unusual is bound to emerge and must then be allowed expression, though with boundaries, to prevent the energy spiralling out of control. The Aquarian mind holds a natural connection with this source and is constantly seeking new ways in which to express that energy.

Friendships are important to Aquarians, though they tend to avoid alliances that are clingy, needy, restrictive or overly demanding. Independence is paramount. They prefer to steer their own course and, if this is opposed or blocked, they rebel against those who hold them back. Their free-thinking minds can make them a mystery to other, more conventional, types, and their quirks and eccentricities are viewed as interesting or odd, depending upon the observer.

The relationship between Uranus and his offspring is an apt illustration for the reluctance of Aquarians to kowtow to authority. His children rebelled against him and were unruly and difficult, refusing to be judged by his standards. Uranus' response to their attempts to assert control over him was to detach himself utterly from them, to 'bury' them out of sight and out of mind. The Aquarian energy dislikes being contained or restrained and reacts strongly against any attempts by others to do this. Relationships can have an impersonal edge to them, as Aquarians, though enjoying stimulating company, need the freedom to roam the vast inner regions of the mind. They can then bring the gifts they find back to the earthly, worldly realm and anchor the thoughts into tangible, usable forms.

CHAPTER TEN

Neptune ♆
Poseidon

Poseidon guards his secrets closely, hides them in the numinous realm of the subconscious. Dreams and nightmares, visions and illusions are his domain. The mind that seeks to go beyond these, to discover the truth behind the seductive trappings of maya, must first dive into Poseidon's realm and risk all to bring the pearl of wisdom to the surface. Too shallow a dive and only confusion awaits: too deep, and madness beckons. Poseidon makes his own rules, and breaks them when he wishes to.

Yet make a friend of this elusive god and gateways into mystery are opened. The ecstasy of spiritual communion, the wordless song of the self is reached when Poseidon chooses to turn the key and allow access to the deep self.

The Birth of Poseidon

Poseidon was one of the sons of Cronus and Rhea. In the best-known version of the myths, he was swallowed by Cronus at birth and was later rescued when Zeus challenged his father and forced him, with potent herbs provided by Metis, to regurgitate his siblings. The three brothers drew lots for the realms and Poseidon won the sea and from then onwards ruled the waves. His emblems became the white horse, the bull and the trident. White horses with golden manes drew his chariot over the sea and he used his trident to stir up the waves to a frenzy, creating storms, when he was angry. The bull reflects his stubborn nature.

There is another version of the birth of Poseidon, however. In this, Rhea substituted a foal for the newborn child but Cronus, realising this, took Poseidon and threw him into the sea, expecting him to drown. Instead, he survived and the waters became his domain.

Personality Traits

Poseidon was a tempestuous god. Like the sea, he could be peaceful, but often he was violent and vengeful, with a tendency to quarrel with others and to seek retribution if he did not get his own way. He brought forth raging storms that destroyed all in their path, would deprive areas of water if he was offended (and he was easily offended), and was a fearful opponent. When in a calmer frame of mind, he would lull the waves and dissipate storms by riding his chariot over the sea, pulled by white horses. Even now, the frothy crests of waves are called 'white horses' in remembrance of him.

He grew fierce if he found that he had been deceived. When King Minos of Crete asked Poseidon for help, the god sent a white bull from the waves, stipulating that it was to be sacrificed to him. But the bull was so beautiful that Minos sacrificed another in its stead and hid the bull away. The god, in revenge, caused Minos' wife, Pasiphae, to fall in love with the beast and mate with it. From this union came the Minotaur, a fierce creature that was half-man, half-bull and demanded human flesh. King Minos built a labyrinth as a home for the bull and each year sent young men and women as sacrifices to the creature. Eventually, with the help of Aphrodite and Minos' daughter, Ariadne, Theseus entered the labyrinth armed with a sword and a ball of golden twine and slew the Minotaur. When he abandoned Ariadne, Aphrodite took revenge on his family, creating a tragedy that Poseidon was drawn into, by sending a wave to sweep Theseus' son to his death in the sea.

The name 'Poseidon' derives from 'posis Da', meaning 'husband of the earth'. As well as the sea itself, Poseidon ruled shifts within the earth and could cause earthquakes. His sovereignty over underground springs enabled him to nourish the earth from beneath – or, when enraged, to flood it. His earlier name as husband of the earth bears connotations of a pre-Olympian god who was worshipped in pagan traditions as a consort of the earth goddess.

Although feared by gods and men for his rages and his ability to hold grudges over lengthy periods of time, Poseidon had a gentler side to his nature. He favoured Castor and Pollux, twin sons of Zeus and Leda, who were conceived after Zeus seduced Leda in the form of a swan. When Castor died, he was sent to the underworld realm of Hades, and Pollux was taken to Olympus. But Pollux mourned the loss of his twin so deeply that the gods took pity on them and made them both immortal. They agreed to divide their time between the underworld and Olympus, and Poseidon made them both guardians of sailors. Eventually they were set in the heavens, with a constellation named after them and are now known as Gemini, the Twins.

In the southern corner of the world of Ancient Greece lived the Aethiopians, people of harmony and tranquillity whose feasts were legendary. Poseidon, deeply touched at the feasts held in his name, visited the Aethiopians to relax and surround himself in their gentle energy.

He was a complex god, ruled by his emotions and, like Ares, disliked by his fellow Olympians because he expressed his feelings forcefully rather than adopting a cooler, more logical stance. The sea, his domain, represents the emotional life as well as the unconscious and reflects his many moods, which ranged from turbulent and violent to still and calm.

Ruler of the Deep

Even when the surface of the sea appears to be peaceful, the depths are unknowable. No light reaches the seabed and there are still areas that are inaccessible, even with modern technology. The pressure is intense, capable of crushing us out of existence, and strange creatures inhabit the darkness. Poseidon was the only god to have access to this domain and he preferred to keep its mysteries silent and secret. The emotional resonance that Poseidon holds is illustrated in the saying that 'still waters run deep'. Yet he could ride the waves, driving his chariot to soothe them or stir them into a frenzied, deathly dance. Like the sea, there was an unfathomable quality to him, and the god and the sea even now keep many of their monsters and treasures hidden where none can reach them.

The subconscious mind is the resting place for the monsters that lurk within the psyche; the home of primeval fears that colour our minds with hues so subtle that we only notice them when they exert control over the way we live our lives. But there are gifts and treasures here also. The creatures of the deep create their own forms of light and find their own way by it. They inhabit a world that we can only imagine, that allows us entry through the vision-making faculties of the mind, fuelled by the deep emotions that open portals into the deep self.

Relationships

Poseidon, like most of the gods, had many lovers. He fell in love with Amphitrite and when she hid from him he pursued her to ask her to be his wife. Delphinus, the dolphin, interceded and pleaded Poseidon's cause and Amphitrite agreed to marry the god. In gratitude, Poseidon placed Delphinus among the stars as a constellation.

The marriage of Poseidon and Amphitrite was similar to that of Zeus and Hera. His frequent straying made Amphitrite so enraged that she, like Hera, took revenge on the women whom her husband lusted after. A few escaped her vigilant eye. Demeter, out searching for her daughter Persephone when Hades had abducted her, was pursued by Poseidon and transformed herself into a mare so that she could hide in a herd of horses. Poseidon took on the form of a stallion and mated with her.

Poseidon and Amphitrite had a son and two daughters, and he sired numerous children by other women – some of them monsters who inherited his more vindictive qualities. Like Ares, he was devoted to his sons, and always took their side.

Sibling Rivalry

Poseidon was a jealous god. He coveted the throne of Zeus and frequently attempted to overthrow his brother but was always defeated. In one tale he enlisted the support of Hera and Athena when Zeus was out of favour with them and they helped him to chain Zeus up, but the leader of the gods broke free and Poseidon returned to his watery realm.

His relationship with Athena was usually stormy. Her coolness infuriated him, and his temper made her hostile. When he seduced Medusa, a beautiful young woman, in a temple of Athena's, the furious goddess turned Medusa into a monstrous gorgon with snakes for hair. Looking upon her would turn mortals to stone. The unfortunate woman was later slain by the hero Perseus, son of Zeus and Danae, who was conceived when Zeus visited Danae as a golden shower. Athena advised Perseus to use his shield as a mirror in order to avoid being turned to stone by gazing directly at Medusa's face. When he beheaded her, the winged horse, Pegasus, sprang from her neck; his relationship to Poseidon, with his equine connection, was apparent.

Poseidon competed with Athena for rulership of the city of Athens and both bequeathed a gift in order to persuade the citizens to choose them. Athena gave an olive tree, while Poseidon donated a spring. The citizens chose Athena, and Poseidon, in a rage, sent a flood to surround the city.

His ability to control underground springs and earthquakes was a source of deep worry to Hades, who feared that the roof of the underworld would collapse and destroy his domain.

Archetypal Resonance

Poseidon as an archetype embodies the realm of deep emotion and bears a darker aspect to the desire for love symbolised by Aphrodite, of whom he is an archetypal harmonic. The ability to dive beneath the surface, to go beyond outward forms and engage intuitively with unplumbed areas of the mind and feelings that are not easily accessible, is the gift of Poseidon. This can appear as a curse or a blessing. The emotions can be overwhelmed, out of their depth, if no constructive channel can be found for their expression. Poseidon was governed by his feelings and released them in torrents of rage or waves of love and creativity. He demanded respect, which does not come easily in many cultures, ancient or modern, where excessive displays of emotion are frowned upon. Yet this access to the regions of the mind that are dark and fathomless, illuminated by creatures who have never seen the light of day, enables you to tap into and discover the mysteries of the inner self. These regions are sensed rather than seen; they can be terrifying or profound, depending upon your willingness to acknowledge and permit their presence in the psyche.

This intensity can allow entry into the numinous realms of inspiration and creativity. The deepest regions of the mind are interpreted through symbols, the language of the subconscious, and an intuitive connection with these gives rise to an understanding of our inner nature and to the expression of this through poetry, music and mysticism.

The positive aspect of the Poseidon archetype is the gentle, dreamy mystic; a clear, uncluttered conduit that the muse can be channelled through. Intensity of feeling brings about great highs and lows, but from these come tremendous insights and a plethora of artistic expression that more earthy types are touched by. As a higher energetic octave to Aphrodite, whose birth took place within his realm, this element of Poseidon brings a deep sense of compassion and empathy, and a connection with an inner wellspring that pours forth directly from the source of life.

In its negative form, the Poseidon archetype manifests as repressed emotion that, when the limits of containment have been breached, has no alternative but to burst forth as rages or fits of weeping. Because Poseidon is the shadow aspect of Zeus, feeling supersedes logic and there are frequent experiences of loss or defeat over issues of power, ownership, or leadership. Those who oppose Poseidon are left to deal with an implacable and vindictive enemy.

Another expression of Poseidon is as the wild, instinctual masculine force that intuits situations and cannot be put in a mould or tamed. The power that Poseidon holds over us is fuelled by strength and courage and is as tumultuous as the sea, making us fearless about facing opponents, even in defeat.

The Qualities of Neptune

The planet Neptune is an appropriate astronomical mirror for the Greek Poseidon and his Roman counterpart. From a distance this gas giant, with its atmosphere of helium and hydrogen, appears blue, with fluffy white clouds, but its weather systems, like the surface of the sea, are all that can be seen of the surface of the planet. Beneath those clouds are gases and liquids that seethe and boil. Storms and hurricanes rage across the planet, carrying winds that reach up to 730 miles (1,170 kilometres) an hour. Dark spots are visible through the atmosphere, marking the presence of storms of unimaginable velocity and fury. These are thought to be hurricanes, each containing an eye in its midst that opens into areas of the atmosphere that cannot be seen from above the planet. One year on Neptune is the equivalent to 164 Earth years; time moves slowly in the realms of the immortals.

As with Jupiter, more heat is generated within Neptune than is received from the Sun. Neptune produces twice as much energy as it is bequeathed by the distant star that it orbits. Astronomers theorise that this arises through a process whereby Neptune contracts through the force of its own gravity, which stirs up the interior of the planet and creates the intense movement of the clouds that sweep past high above.

These characteristics reflect much of the mythology of Poseidon: the unknowable qualities, the storms that rage within, the hurricanes whose eyes look downwards into mystery. Like the god himself, the planet refuses to give away too many of its secrets. And in the calmer regions, it is the dazzling blue of the sea on a calm day, where clouds galloping across like white horses leave only traces of their passing.

In Your Natal Chart

The placement of Neptune in your natal chart indicates how you experience and express the deep emotions, and how you access the image-making faculties of the mind. The nebulous qualities of the planet and the god bring increased intuition, depth of feeling, premonitions and mystical insights through Poseidon's rulership of the subconscious mind. From these depths emerge symbols that can be interpreted and understood. Poseidon allows his secrets to unveil themselves if you are willing to dive deep and be amazed by, rather than afraid of, what you see.

When suppressed by difficult planetary aspects, Neptune manifests either as sudden rages and eruptions when frustrations are encountered, or as a state of introversion in which the feelings are buried deep below the surface and are not allowed credence until they boil over and create havoc.

But when channelled constructively, Neptune brings a connection with inner space, with a luminous source that enables glimpses of beauty in all forms. Surfaces are penetrated, and even the apparently mundane is seen to have a magical place in the world.

The longing to penetrate mysteries that is facilitated by Neptune can, if not allowed expression, become an urge towards escapism, particularly through the abuse of alcohol and drugs. The experiences these offer are illusory and, like the negative aspect of the god, devious. They provide only a temporary sense of connection with the deep self and ultimately become a trap that drives you further from your true nature.

Yet when tapped into through meditation, visualisation, use of imagery or creativity, Neptune bestows the gifts of insight and compassion. Artists and film makers tend to have a strong Neptunian connection, indicated by their ability to envision and understand how the mind works and to create symbolic repre-sentations of imagery that others can relate to at a feeling level.

As a deity, Poseidon was shunned, misunderstood and even feared by his family. His unpredictability, his longing for acceptance – which led him to attempt to gain power through grasping what others had in order to be viewed as similar – proved unfulfilling and frustrating. A strong Neptune influence in the natal chart can best be expressed through an acceptance of differences, and an appreciation of the potential of the gifts at hand. The most beautiful works of art are those that emerge through passionate emotion. The most inspirational people are those who are in tune with their positive Neptunian qualities – who are not afraid to be different, and who allow their voices to soar freely above the humdrum drone of conventionality.

Rulership of Neptune

Neptune rules the astrological sign Pisces. The symbol of two fish swimming in opposite directions reflects the dual nature of Neptune – the turbulent, manipulative nature that uses tears as a weapon, and the compassionate mystic whose empathy breeds altruism and gentleness. Both of these elements are present in the

Piscean nature, although one will be more dominant than the other, depending upon the position of the planet in the natal chart. Their watery nature makes Pisceans sensitive and ruled by their emotions. The symbol of the fish also illustrates an element of indecision in the Piscean make-up. Their desire to go with the flow, and their innate sympathy towards others can make them indecisive about which direction is the best to move in. They are patient and kind, but when provoked beyond their limits can display astonishing outbursts of emotion.

A tendency towards mood swings is marked, with displays of the heights of optimism followed by the depths of pessimism. This unpredictability is emphasised by the Neptunian link with the sea, which can be calm one moment and engulfed by stormy waves soon after. The Piscean need for retreat to a place of peace and solitude in order to gather their energy and equanimity reflects Poseidon's delight in the sanctuary of Aethiopia.

They can appear dreamy and otherworldly, impelled by internal visions that those around them find difficult to decipher, and they dislike being pinned down and cast into a mould that is set by others. Their imagination is active and fertile and their visionary faculties are strong. This can manifest as artistic or poetic abilities, or through sculpture and dance. The Poseidon influence often gives a feeling of needing more control; of not being the master of their own destiny, just as the god attempted to go beyond his own designated boundaries and rule other realms. The boundaries of Pisceans are nebulous, undefined, and it can be difficult for them to know whether what they are feeling comes from within them, or from the people around them.

The Piscean psyche longs to encompass the mysteries of life and to be encompassed by the feelings of homecoming that are generated through a connection with the source. Like Poseidon, they sometimes feel misunderstood, but hold great power within them.

CHAPTER ELEVEN

Pluto
Hades

The essential quality of Hades is access to the underworld of the self; the repository of all that has gone before, the depths of the unconscious, both personal and collective. Here lie the blueprints of all previous experience, with their gifts and terrors and their potential for regeneration.

The dark of Hades' realm is the dark of the earth, where seeds must germinate in solitude and silence before pushing upwards into the light. This dark is fearful only because it is unknown, unfamiliar. It takes what is no longer needed back into itself, pares down the bones of outward forms in order that new, healthy flesh may grow on them. As lord of the dead, Hades opens the portal to the birth of the new self. He allows no looking back, no fond glances towards the past. He bequeaths the awareness that death is only another adventure that leads to rebirth.

The Birth of Hades

Hades was one of the six children of Cronus and Rhea and was swallowed at birth by his father. After Zeus forced Cronus to regurgitate his siblings, Hades joined with Zeus, Poseidon and the

Titans to battle with his father. The victorious brothers then drew lots to divide the universe into three: the heavens, the sea and the underworld. Hades became ruler of the underworld, the realm of shadows.

Personality Traits

Hades was the quietest of the gods. He chose to stay secluded in his realm, and in the Greek myths was known to have left the underworld twice only: once to abduct Persephone and once to travel to Olympus to be healed of a wound inflicted on him by Heracles. He avoided the conflicts and dramas that his family revelled in and had no urge to seek adventures. He owned a cap that could make its wearer invisible and used its powers to retain his privacy, preferring his own company to that of others.

The Greeks were superstitious about using his name, lest they invoked him inadvertently. He inspired awe rather than fear and his titles included 'The Unseen One' and 'The Rich One'. The Romans chose to call him Pluto, a derivative of 'Plouton', another of his names. Plutonium, a chemical element that is a silvery radioactive metal used in atomic physics, is also named after the god, as the planet's discovery marked the beginning of the Atomic age.

Unlike the rest of his family, Hades had few romantic liaisons. His reclusive temperament set him apart. Those who entered his realm, with few notable exceptions, went there because their mortal lives were at an end, and it was rare to leave the underworld and travel back to the light. The god and the domain both bore the same name, and were closely identified with each other.

The psychological realm of Hades is the unconscious mind and encompasses both the collective unconscious (the storehouse of all memory) and the personal unconscious (the repressed memories and thoughts that are only seen and felt as shadows by the conscious mind). The underworld that Hades inhabited was the place where the shades of the dead went to rest. Later, Christians would link the underworld with Hell, named after the Norse goddess Hel, queen of the Nordic underworld. Yet there is no link between the realm of Hades and that of the Christian Devil. Hades, though considered stern and grim by the Greeks, was not viewed as evil or malicious. His realm did not welcome visitors other than those who belonged there, but it was not a fearsome place. And Hades had no interest in the worlds beyond his own. Recluses throughout history have a strong Hades aspect, shunning the company of others in order to maintain their solitude.

Hades was the god of wealth as well as lord of the underworld. The riches hidden deep within the earth — fossil fuels, gemstones, precious metals — belong to him. Although he possessed untold riches, he valued them silently without needing to make showy displays. The god carried his position with silent dignity, except when he fell in love with Persephone.

His rulership of the areas of dark and shadow, of the depths that are negotiated as an initiatory experience, gave him a reputation for being silent, stern and withdrawn. In modern times these states would be considered to be depressive, and Hades certainly lacked a sense of humour. The god and the realm, identified as one, were serious business.

The Realm of the Dead

At the end of mortal life, Hermes would accompany the souls of the dead to the underworld. First the River Styx had to be crossed, and the souls took with them a coin to pay the ferryman who waited there to take them on the next stage of their journey, across the dark water. At the other side were the gates to the underworld, guarded by Cerberus, a massive and terrifying three-headed hound, who allowed entry, but permitted none to leave. Once past the gates, the souls were judged before Minos, Rhadamanthus and Aeacus before being permitted to fully enter Hades' realm.

The shades of the dead remained in the underworld as shadows of their mortal selves. Some stayed forever; others drank from the waters of Lethe, which made them forget all that had gone before, and were reborn again. Hades was divided into three areas. The Plain of Asphodel was the place where most souls were taken. A few fortunate ones went to Elysium, the islands of blessed immortality. Tartarus was the equivalent of the Christian and Buddhist hell-realms, where those who had committed evil deeds were imprisoned and punished.

The entrance to Hades was said to be through the mouth of a cave in an isolated area at the very edge of the world, though Hades could open the earth and disappear into it wherever he chose.

Relationships

The only sexual relationship that Hades had was with Persephone, daughter of his sister Demeter and brother Zeus. He abducted, raped and married her, but Persephone's unwillingness to give herself to him, and her anguish at being taken from her beloved mother, meant that the forced marriage began joylessly. Later, when Hermes came to fetch Persephone, an agreement was forged between husband and wife. Persephone ate seeds from a pomegranate that Hades gave her and kept her promise to divide her year between the underworld and the light.

Before he met Persephone, Hades desired Minthe, but she turned into a mint plant and was lost to him before he could touch her. Another who eluded him was Leuce, who became a white poplar tree. Hades could be content with celibacy, but was also capable of forming deep and enduring attachments, as he did with Persephone despite his initial tawdry treatment of her. His silent, brooding demeanour did not make him skilled at the hearts-and-flowers approach to romance. Hades desired little, but ensured that he took what he wanted. Although his brothers Zeus and Poseidon forced their attentions on women, it is Hades who is renowned and reviled for his treatment of Persephone. With the more extroverted gods, this behaviour was viewed as an aspect of nature, and it was felt that all women were theirs by right of their sovereignty. Because Hades was the quiet god, his obsession with Persephone was more noticeable than the philandering of his brothers. Unlike Zeus and Poseidon, he was faithful to his wife after marriage.

Sibling Rivalry

Hades avoided contact with others, including his siblings, as much as possible. He refused to engage in power struggles, and had no interest in gaining ownership of any domain other than his own. When he abducted Persephone, Zeus pretended not to hear her cries for help as she was taken to the underworld. If his loyalties were to be divided, he was on the side of his brother, and he later ignored the pleas of her mother, Demeter, to intercede and insist on Persephone's freedom.

Poseidon's rages and storms made Hades nervous. He feared that his brother's tempestuous nature would bring down the roof of the underworld and render him without a home and domain. He took his responsibilities as king of the shades seriously, and was aware that if disaster struck there would be no place for the souls of the dead to inhabit.

The other deities viewed Hades as one who was set apart from them, and his lack of interest and solemn nature ensured that he was not included in their activities. Hades was a loner who relished the freedom from strife that his aloofness brought him.

Archetypal Resonance

As god of the underworld, Hades embodies the shadowy aspects of the psyche; the deep, dark, hidden areas of the unconscious mind. If he ventured above the surface he wore his cap of invisibility, which indicates that even when acting at a conscious level the motives remain hidden from those around him. Whereas Poseidon/Neptune is the subconscious aspect of the deep self, which makes itself known through turbulent emotions and intuitive insights, the realm that Hades inhabits is buried beyond the reach of the everyday mind.

This archetype is the strong, silent, brooding element within, who needs peace, quiet and solitude in order to be at home with himself. The darkest Hades area of the psyche holds the key to buried fears and to that which is too shameful or distasteful to be expressed. From their resting place within, these qualities exert an invisible control over external emotions and reactions. Memories are suppressed but not obliterated, and reflect as fragments of associations that outwardly appear insignificant, but unconsciously hold great power.

The Pluto aspect of Hades, as god of wealth, is found in those who have gained riches but reject the social niceties of the outer world. At a more fundamental level, the riches that Hades symbolises are the jewels of soul. A diamond is in truth a chunk of carbon that has been crushed by pressure from within the depths of the earth. Hard enough to resist attempts to smash it, when it is removed from its womb and cut and polished it becomes a highly prized gem of great beauty. The Plutonian aspect of Hades is similar to the diamond, and is accessed through the search for the essential self; for the jewel within. This quest must be undertaken through entering the darkness and silence of Hades, for only through knowing and understanding the shadow can the esoteric realms of the self be fully revealed and integrated.

Experiences of loss and depression drive us downwards into areas that are frightening because the sense of self becomes temporarily lost. Yet the hero element within us must make that descent into the underworld in order to discover hitherto-undreamed-of strengths, and bring these back into the light of everyday life. This is a daunting prospect, because of the fear that once down there in the shadowy dark we will become trapped and unable to return; we will drink the waters of Lethe and forget who we truly are. When we experience despair we see a glimpse of Hades' realm in its interpretation as Hell. Within the domain of this god we are subjected to the thrall of buried fears and desires, impulses and memories that we would prefer to forget. But through this route we can also connect with the root patterns of the archetypal energies that are expressed in our personalities, and can experience a journey of astonishing self-discovery and beauty.

The Qualities of Pluto

Pluto is the smallest planet in our solar system, only two-thirds of the size of our Moon, with an unusual composition, neither gaseous nor rocky. The planet is composed of a form of ice, with jagged ice caps at its poles and a frozen shell of methane covering its surface. This immediate impression bears similarities to the cold, hard, detached reputation of Hades. The planet was discovered in 1930, and this marked the beginning of the Atomic age on Earth. Its Moon, Charon, moves close to Pluto, giving the effect of a double planet rather than a planet with a satellite. This is reminiscent of Hades' relationship with Persephone in their rulership of the underworld, where they were the only living beings among the shades of the dead.

One year on Pluto equals around 248 Earth years. Its orbit is irregular, and as it moves through the constellations that we interpret astrologically, its length of stay in each sign varies between 12 and 32 years. When it reaches its nearest orbital point to the Sun, Pluto warms and some of its atmosphere evaporates into space, making it appear like a comet trailing streams of matter.

In Your Natal Chart

The position of Pluto in your natal chart indicates how you deal with the experiences of symbolic death, regeneration, rebirth, renewal and transformation. This does not relate specifically to physical death, but reflects how we are affected by the endings of cycles in our lives and how we elevate ourselves in order to start afresh. The symbol of the phoenix rising from the ashes is appropriate to Pluto. It represents the death of the old self in the fires of purification and initiation and the fresh flight of the new, elevated self that emerges triumphantly from the ashes of the past. Just as the snake must shed its old, tight skin as it grows, so does Pluto mark the sacred passages that lead to increased self-knowledge.

Because Pluto moves slowly in comparison to Earth time, its influence in the astrological signs is felt as generational rather than personal. Hades' rulership of the collective unconscious is reflected through the movement of the planet through the Sun signs. The influences ripple out through each generation and are felt as what are often seismic shifts in world-view.

Pluto's position in the houses of the natal chart reveals the areas of life in which the facilities for regeneration and transformation are at their most powerful. Pluto in the 2nd house, for instance, reveals the ability to generate riches and a drive to accumulate wealth. In the 7th house, the planet indicates tremendous life-changes arising through relationships and a penetrating ability to understand the minds of others.

Because of Hades' position as both god of the underworld and the underworld as a place, Pluto in the natal chart also concerns conscious willpower and tendencies towards the exploration of hidden meanings. This leads to a desire for self-knowledge through plumbing the depths of the psyche and through the occult, such as esoteric sciences and communion with the dead. When negatively aspected, it can create morbidity, depression, emotional frigidity and a preoccupation with the darker side of life. Issues of control and domination are predominant with negative aspects, as the willpower is strong and is driven to assert itself over others.

When positively aspected, Pluto brings a strength of will that can overcome even apparently insurmountable obstacles. There is no fear of death, which gives the courage to struggle with challenges, because death is viewed as a natural element in the cycles of life. Whereas Ares, through the planet Mars, is courageous to the point of foolhardiness, Pluto is steely-willed and coldly determined to win through. The talent for regeneration that is bestowed through positive aspects to Pluto manifests as the ability to rise from knocks that would seem impossible to survive and to use traumatic experiences as stepping-stones to growth.

A strong Pluto engenders an intense desire to explore regions, particularly those of the mind, where none have gone before. Psychology, investigations into human nature, and a fascination with the occult because of the inner terrain that becomes accessible, are all elements of the Plutonian nature.

The Hades/Pluto connection carries connotations of associations with death and so the position of Pluto can indicate money or possessions that are gained through inheritances. Taxes are another aspect of Pluto. Your ability to acquire and accumulate wealth is also revealed through the area of the natal chart that Pluto rests in.

When Pluto is prominent in the natal chart, the eyes have a compelling, hypnotic quality. This intensity of gaze can make some people feel uncomfortable, because it appears that you can 'see through' them to underlying thoughts and motivations, but the Plutonian gaze can also be extraordinarily compelling.

Rulership of Pluto

Pluto rules the astrological sign Scorpio and is symbolised by the scorpion and the eagle. The scorpion, with its power to instil fear and its lethal sting, represents the connection with the shadow aspect of the underworld and with death. The eagle symbolises the ability of the self to regenerate, to allow the mind to fly free and soar high above in order to see from a unique and far-sighted perspective. The dual nature of this sign, with its potential for plumbing the depths and attaining the dizziest heights, is part of the mystery of Scorpio.

This astrological sign is viewed as the most powerful in the zodiac. Ruled by Pluto, with a deep connection to the underworld of the unconscious mind, and co-ruled by Mars, with the Arian drive and the double dose of force of will bequeathed by both planets, these archetypes are both forces to be reckoned with. Added to this is the exaltation of the planet Uranus in Scorpio, with its attendant insights and magnetic electrical charges of energy. The potential for transformation through the forces that Scorpio contains is awesome.

Because of the links with desire, death and rebirth, there are powerful sexual impulses that can lead to possessiveness and strong romantic attachments. As in the story of Hades and Persephone, the Scorpionic nature is driven by an urge to conquer the object of desire. The symbolic relationship between sex and death, with its connotations of merging into unity and release, is strongly felt in Scorpios and this drive can be acted out physically, or transmuted into an overwhelming need to explore the secrets of life; to discover who we are and why we are here. This can be channelled through mystical research and experiences, or through the esoteric sciences. The current quest in quantum physics to discover the Holy Grail of purpose in life is strongly influenced by Scorpio and Pluto. The deeper the sciences delve into the subatomic worlds, the realms of Hades, the more mysterious the findings become. What was once viewed as the smallest component in the universe, the atom, has proved to be yet another universe, with ever more subtle inhabitants. As this journey moves further into the complexities of inner space, the jewels that come to light become increasingly more exhilarating and intriguing because each discovery opens up new and astonishing realms that each appear to contain a consciousness of their own. As with the treasures hidden in the earth, careful digging is necessary before their secrets can be excavated and deciphered.

The Scorpio nature is immensely resourceful and, because this is a fixed sign, there is also tremendous staying power. 'Never say "die"' is a Scorpio motto, and people who are strongly influenced by this sign are determined to achieve their goals through a combination of strength of will and a refusal to give up. Superficiality is anathema to Scorpios, as they are impelled by an overwhelming urge to dig below the surface and to uncover the reality of any situation that they encounter.

This strength enables them to battle against all odds and to use their secretive nature as a cloak that both protects them and prevents others from knowing them too intimately. Although they refuse to admit weaknesses in themselves and strive to overcome shortcomings, their understanding of the underlying motivations in human nature makes them thoughtful and compassionate when they see other people struggling. They will endeavour to help others as long as a bargain is struck in which the other party is also willing to help themselves. They have little patience or tolerance for 'quitters'.

Diplomacy is not one of Scorpios' virtues and they will remain silent rather than utter an untruth. What matters is the essence that lies at the core of experience; the understanding and insights that can be gained and the effects that these will have in the long term.

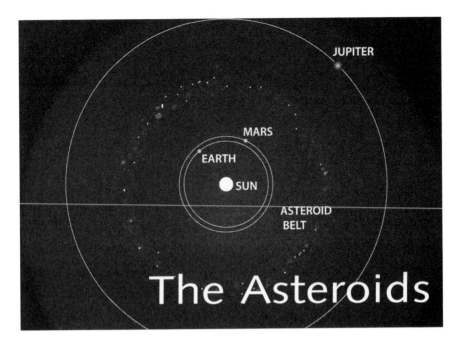

The Asteroids

The asteroid belt is located between Mars and Jupiter and contains over a million asteroids that measure more than a kilometre across. The largest is Ceres, with a diameter of 630 miles (1,000 kilometres). The brightest is Vesta, whose molten core once erupted through volcanoes and spilled lava across its surface.

The asteroids were discovered in around 1800 and the first four to be seen were named Ceres, Pallas Athene, Juno and Vesta, after the Roman goddesses. These stemmed from the Greek Demeter, Athena, Hera and Hestia, the early Olympians. Chiron was discovered later, in 1977, and generated much excitement. Situated between Saturn and Uranus, it was at first thought to be a planet. When a coma, a trail of gas and dust, became visible trailing in its wake, it was demoted to a comet, with possibilities of being an asteroid. Nowadays it is more frequently known as a planetoid, a small planet, measuring 120 miles (190 kilometres) across, with a 51-year orbit around the Sun.

It is postulated that the asteroids are the remains of a planet that disintegrated in the distant past; possibly a planet in the initial stages of formation that was destroyed by the gravitational pull of Jupiter.

The geological properties of the asteroids are certainly similar to those of planets, as are chemical traces left behind by reactions that took place within them in the distant past.

Astrology needs the asteroids and Chiron if the natal chart is to be interpreted fully. They represent, respectively, the female archetypes that are missing in the traditional view, and the male archetype of wisdom and healing. Without them, the feminine is allocated the role of virginal mother (the Moon/Artemis) or lover (Venus/Aphrodite). This does not allow balance within the female psyche or within the inner feminine of the male psyche. The wife (Juno/Hera), the earth mother (Ceres/Demeter), the warlike active thinker (Pallas Athene/Athena), and the light-bearer and mystic (Vesta/Hestia), when included, enable a rounded, more holistic view. The wise and benevolent teacher and healer is portrayed by Chiron, the tutor to gods and heroes, whose skills in medicine, music, hunting and warfare were highly respected.

Rulership of the asteroids is a subject that is still frequently under debate. Signs such as Virgo, which shares Mercury with Gemini, and Scorpio, which has Mars and Pluto as rulers, hold particularly strong resonances with more than one asteroid. The characteristics of the astrological signs often carry connections with several archetypes, depending upon which elements of them are expressed. Human nature is complex and the personalities of the deities reflect this. You can liken this to the function of a violin string that contains the potential for many notes and sings out specific notes depending upon where and how pressure is put on it.

In the symphony of the natal chart the voices of the asteroids also have their places. If we listen to them and allow them to blend their subtle harmonies with the rest, we can attain increased psychological balance and a clearer view of our purpose.

CHAPTER TWELVE

Chiron ⚷
Chiron

The essential nature of Chiron is wisdom through experience. The suffering that this god endured acted as a spur to innovation, to compassion and altruism, to sacrifice, and ultimately to healing and rebirth.

As the wounded healer, Chiron is the symbol of courage, determination and unselfishness. Able to ease the suffering of others while helpless to cure himself, his journey led him to discover that only through releasing and relinquishing can the spirit truly be free to experience its immortality.

The archetype of the healer manifests through Chiron as the recognition that matter and energy are inextricably interconnected. He reminds us that the source of healing must be sought before progression can be made. As with the homeopathic principle of 'like cures like', Chiron reminds us that only through recognising and accepting our inner wounds can we find true healing.

The Birth of Chiron

Chiron was the son of Cronus and Philyra and was conceived before Zeus challenged his father and rescued his siblings. In her flight from Cronus, Philyra turned herself into a horse in order to gain speed. But Cronus transformed himself into a stallion, caught up with her and mated with her. The result of their union was Chiron, whose physiology was that of a centaur: half-man, half-horse.

Philyra, appalled at the sight of the creature she had birthed, abandoned him and begged the gods to release her from her mortal form. Her pleas were answered and she was turned into a linden tree, whose healing blossoms are used to promote sleep. This signifies her refusal to 'wake up' to the situation she found herself in.

Chiron became renowned for his wisdom and for his skills in medicine, the arts, divination, hunting and warfare. Whereas the other centaurs were fond of rough pursuits and debauchery, Chiron made his home in a cave in Thessaly and followed a higher path. He taught Apollo to play the lyre that he had won from Hermes, and became tutor to Apollo's son Asclepius, passing on his knowledge of healing. When Asclepius raised a mortal from the dead, Hades complained to Zeus, fearing that the underworld would lose its population, and Zeus killed Asclepius with a thunderbolt.

Other heroes, including the archetypal Achilles and Jason, were mentored by Chiron and learned many of their skills from him. When Chiron died, Zeus placed him in the heavens as the constellation Centaurus.

Personality Traits

Chiron was rejected by both of his parents. Philyra found his appearance abhorrent and Cronus was too busy trying to keep his power from being taken by his children with Rhea. Because of this he grew up alone and unloved, isolated from those he needed to feel close to. His energy was channelled into learning the skills that he became teacher of, and his intelligence and compassion, born of suffering, marked him out as an inspired counsellor, healer and tutor, and a devoted friend.

His wisdom was said to be a gift from Athena, bequeathed when she laid her hand on his forehead. He was generous with his knowledge, and gods and mortals benefited equally from it. All who came to him for healing or tuition were deeply touched by him. He was greatly loved for his gentle spirit and unselfishness, as well as for his skills, but he was set apart by his differences from his fellow centaurs and from mortals and gods.

Chiron's understanding of herb lore was profound and he continually discovered and developed new ways in which to facilitate the healing process. Yet when these skills were needed for himself, he could not effect the cure he sought. It is this facet of his nature that is most strongly emphasised in his archetypal and astrological resonances.

The Wounded Healer

There are two wounds associated with Chiron. The first is emotional, as a result of the rejection he suffered from both parents at birth. The second was physical and accidental.

Chiron was inflicted with a terrible wound that poisoned him and made him suffer greatly. Because he was an immortal, he could not die of it, much as he wished to release himself from the painful prison that his body became. Ultimately it was an altruistic act that set him free and allowed him to die.

There are several versions of the story of how Chiron received his bodily wound. In one, he was struck accidentally by a spear that left a wound that would not heal. In another a poisoned arrow that he was removing from an injured centaur pricked him. A third story tells how Heracles unintentionally wounded him in battle. The wound festered and caused him tremendous agony that, try as he might, he could not escape from. This drove him to find ever more effective ways of healing the sick, yet although these worked on others, he was immune to everything that he used on himself. The knowledge of his immortality and the horror of living through eternity in constant pain led him to make a decision to die by offering himself in the place of Prometheus, who had been cast out by the gods.

Prometheus was the son of the Titan Iapetus, one of the early gods. He took the side of Zeus when, with the help of the Titans, he overthrew his father, Cronus. But he fell from favour with Zeus because of his love of mortals, which Zeus considered to be beneath his station. Zeus had hidden fire, in the view that it was too potent to be used by others, but Prometheus stole it and gave it to the mortals. In his fury, Zeus sent Prometheus to Tartarus, the realm of the underworld where the wicked were imprisoned and tortured. There he was chained to a rock and left to eternal torment.

Each day an eagle tore out his liver and each night it grew whole again. This was enacted day after day. Trapped there and abandoned by his kin, it seemed that there would be no end to his suffering.

But Chiron interceded. He begged to be permitted to take the place of Prometheus. Zeus agreed, Prometheus was released and Chiron was chained to the rock. After nine days he died, and Zeus placed him in the heavens as the constellation Centaurus.

Relationships

Chiron joined the other centaurs in some of their revelries, but avoided becoming involved in their lustiness and lived quietly in his cave on Mount Pelion in Thessaly. He was greatly loved, and inspired respect through his qualities of kindness and generosity. As tutor to gods and mortals he gave of himself unstintingly and passed on whichever skills were sought, whether in medicine and healing, or in warfare.

Athena was fond of Chiron, to the extent of gifting him with her own energy and adding to his innate wisdom. Apollo thought highly of him and in some stories became his benefactor and guardian when he was abandoned by his parents – though this tale is rather unlikely chronologically, as Chiron was born before Zeus overthrew Cronus, and Apollo was a son of Zeus.

There was no significant lover in Chiron's life. His role as a priest-like figure to the centaurs, and as a being whose focus was on the needs of others, meant that his own needs were somewhat neglected. His sense of self was damaged through his rejection by his parents, and the theme of Chiron carries an underlying sadness, despite his willingness to give of himself to others. The relationships that he engaged in were ones in which he was very much the giver rather than the receiver. As the wise one, the tutor, healer, astrologer and sage, his time and energy were devoted to the well-being of all who entered his sphere.

Siblings

Chiron had no full-blood siblings, but the children of Cronus were his half-brothers and sisters. His heritage was tightly bound in with the Titans – the primal nature gods and goddesses who brought all manner of strange creatures to birth. Although he was unlike his relatives, the relationships that Chiron engaged in were benign; his altruistic nature made him a source of pleasure to those who sought him out.

Archetypal Resonance

Chiron as an archetype embodies the shaman, the wounded healer and teacher who is the link between body, mind and spirit and who, through his skills and actions, perpetuates the healing of those around him. The suffering that Chiron endured was not of his own creation – neither his abandonment by his parents, which left an internal emotional wound, nor the external wound caused by the poisoned arrow were self-inflicted. But these experiences led him to seek new methods of healing. The wounds became the blueprint for Chiron's archetypal resonance because both stemmed from trust;

the trust of a child that his parents would love and care for him and the trust as a healer that good will come about through helping others. Chiron's wounds were healed through making the ultimate sacrifice – that of himself – and that surrender led him to a state of healing and wholeness.

As half-man, half-horse, Chiron embodies the connection between the instinctual, unconscious mind and the intellectual, philosophical, conscious mind. A synthesis between these is a necessary prerequisite for wisdom. Without instinct, philosophising is purely cerebral, detached from the nitty-gritty of everyday life. The combination of both of these elements creates a profound search for, and understanding of, what gives meaning to our lives.

Chiron's inability to heal himself is reflected in life through the areas in which we can be useful to others through recognising and coming to terms with our own inner wound. Despite his pain he refused to give up or give in. Instead, this spurred him to discover new forms of healing that could benefit others. His wound prompted him to reach out and use his skills to their fullest in order to be of service to others who were in need. This archetype is prominent in people whose suffering, either through loss or illness, motivates them to train in counselling or in some form of healing, or to set up organisations and support groups that provide help and an exchange of information.

In one of the versions of Chiron's wounding, the cause was an arrow shot by Heracles, which accidentally struck Chiron. This has tremendous significance in the ultimate healing and subsequent placing of Chiron in the heavens, for it was Heracles who interceded on Chiron's behalf and persuaded Zeus to allow Chiron to take the place of Prometheus in Tartarus. This implies that it is the cause of the initial wound that provides the facility for healing to take place. The wound itself was not healed, but the cause, the perpetrator, of this was eventually the means by which release from pain was accomplished.

An element of sacrifice is clear in Chiron's archetypal resonance. His physical wound was received through his intercession on behalf of others. He was willing to risk all in order to be of service. His solution to his own suffering was to relieve the agony of Prometheus by taking his place – to save a life through offering up his own life. Through this act he attained release and regained the state of immortality. When we take action on behalf of others, with no thought for the repercussions on ourselves, we are connecting with Chiron. When we face a choice in which a sacrifice must be made in order to attain our goal, Chiron's voice can be heard within the psyche. Ultimately, the path we take through the decisions we make leads to the higher good.

In Your Natal Chart

The position of Chiron in the natal chart reveals the area in which we carry an inner wound that has the potential to become our greatest gift. This prompts a search for healing that facilitates wholeness within ourselves and enables us to reach out to others and touch them deeply. Chiron's astronomical position, between Saturn and Uranus, represents the bridge between the oppression that is felt by inner needs that are not being met and the unusual and unexpected solution that leads to freedom.

The path to healing that is mapped out through Chiron's position in the natal chart is gained through acceptance. The area in which Chiron rests represents the focus for our feelings of rejection or pain at the hands of others. Chiron's unique relationship with gods and mortals, and his abilities as a wise one and teacher, came about in part because of his underlying aloneness. His early rejection created a sense of isolation, of not belonging. He avoided the coarse behaviour of the other centaurs, yet was not mortal. His place was that of intermediary, using his considerable gifts, born of suffering, to help others. In return he was blessed with great wisdom, which gave him a status that gods and mortals both recognised.

Wounds are an aspect of life. We cannot pass through life unscathed, because the experience of feeling opens up avenues to rejection and pain. Yet through these we become compassionate, empathetic and sympathetic. Our own suffering creates an ability to understand that of others and to use our resources to be of help.

Negative aspects to Chiron indicate blocks that stand in the way of healing. These can drain the energy through emotional experiences of despair and hopelessness and a lack of self-acceptance. This makes the challenge to manifest the positive aspects of Chiron more difficult to work with. Yet these blocks themselves are often the key to resolution, just as Chiron's wound impelled him to discover more about healing methods. There can be a view of the self as either the wounded victim or the perpetrator of wounds on others, if no attempts are made to examine the causes of these attitudes and find a way to work constructively with them.

Positive aspects to Chiron reveal the forces that can be accessed in building the bridge between the instinctual mind and the spiritual self. These indicate the potential to also create bridges between the self and others and to grow through developing the capacity for nurturing and accumulating wisdom.

Rulership of Chiron

There is much debate between astrologers over which sign is ruled by Chiron. On one side of the arena stands Sagittarius, which is represented by the image of the Centaur with his bow and arrow and who expresses himself philosophically and spiritually. The Sagittarian nature accords with Chiron's quality of active intelligence, which leads them to wish to pass on their gifts to others through teaching what they know. In his rulership of Sagittarius, Chiron carries the instrument of his own wound (the arrow) and must use his insight and intelligence to discover how healing can be facilitated.

The quality of aloofness, of looking down from above that can be seen in Sagittarians, coupled with an innate friendliness, honesty and openness, resonates strongly with the personal demeanour of Chiron, as does the quest for knowledge and truth that is a driving force in this sign.

Virgoans also claim a right to rulership by Chiron and hold some convincing arguments in their favour. The aspects of healing, service and sacrifice that Chiron embodies are very Virgoan.

The Virgoan impulse towards maintaining inner and outer health through associations with holistic forms of medicine is further accentuated by Virgo's need to be of service to others. The Virgoan intellect, purity and self-effacing qualities, Virgos' diffidence about putting themselves forward and their willingness to sacrifice their own needs in order to fulfil those of others, are qualities that resonate strongly with those of Chiron.

The Sagittarian intellect is geared towards the accumulation of knowledge through study and education, through formal bodies of learning such as colleges and universities. The Virgoan intelligence is more earthy. Wisdom is sought and gained through direct experience in the 'university of life', which again is closer to the manner in which Chiron discovered the skills that he then honed and developed through experimentation.

When Chiron was first discovered, Virgoans heaved a sigh of relief and staked their claim. At last it seemed that their ruling planet had appeared, allowing the qualities in Virgo to be more fully expressed and realised. As the debate continues over which sign Chiron truly rules, only time, of which Chiron, through Cronus, is the son, will allow the evidence for each astrological sign to be clarified, and provide a firm conclusion.

CHAPTER THIRTEEN

Ceres ⚳
Demeter

Demeter, as the embodiment of the earth mother, is defined through her relationship with her daughter, Persephone, and with the land. Her fertility is expressed through both. An earth mother is one who nurtures her offspring, surrounds them with love and support, and protects them from harm. Yet children grow up and leave home, and the earth mother must then find other outlets for this fecund energy; or, like Demeter, they pine away in the absence of their children.

The focus of Demeter is purely upon her daughter. Without her there is no channel for joy or creativity, and winter descends upon the emotional life. Yet within each winter, the seeds sleep, awaiting the warm touch of springtime.

The Birth of Demeter

As a daughter of Cronus and Rhea, Demeter was swallowed at birth by her father and later retrieved when Zeus defeated Cronus and administered a powerful herbal emetic. Whereas her brothers divided the realms of sky, sea and underworld between them, Demeter became goddess of the earth and all growing things.

Her symbol was grain and specifically corn. It was she who woke the earth and encouraged it to produce, and she was kind and sympathetic towards mortals, who revered her as the source of all nourishment. Demeter taught mortals how to grow and harvest crops in order to feed themselves and their livestock, and was associated with abundance and fertility. As goddess of fecundity and abundance she was depicted carrying a sheaf of grains and poppies; the wheat symbolised the gifts of the earth, and poppies represented death and rebirth.

As the devoted earth mother, Demeter's story is inextricably linked with that of her daughter by Zeus, Persephone, who was called Kore by the Romans. Her close relationship with her daughter was the cause of the seasons and of the Eleusinian Rites, which were performed each year retelling the story of the love of mother and daughter for each other, the loss that both were subjected to, and their eventual reconciliation.

Persephone and Demeter

Persephone was a beautiful young woman and devoted to her mother, who loved her beyond all else. The two were inseparable and, although Persephone had many suitors, she chose to remain single and stay by the side of Demeter. Lovely in both appearance and temperament, malleable and acquiescent, Persephone was the embodiment of the innocent maiden: untouched, pure of spirit and with no thought of fear or danger.

While she strolled with her maidens through the Nysian fields, plucking flowers for her mother, she strayed from Demeter's sight, unaware that she was being observed by Hades, who had fallen in love with her. Hades, determined to have her as his wife and lacking the finesse of her other suitors, burst forth from the earth in his chariot drawn by black horses, swept Persephone away and, deaf to her screams for help, took her with him into the underworld. There he raped and married her.

Zeus had witnessed his daughter's abduction but, feeling that it was time she married and considering Hades to be a worthy husband for her, ignored her cries and allowed Hades to take her. The earth that had opened to allow Hades through closed behind them and they vanished.

When Demeter discovered that Persephone had disappeared, she searched the Earth for her, crying out her name. She refused to eat or sleep and tore her clothes to rags and covered herself in dirt. Zeus turned away from her pleas to bring her daughter back and, in anguish, Demeter left Olympus and wandered the Earth as an ancient beggar-woman. An attempt was made to rescue Persephone. Theseus and Pirithous made their way secretly into the underworld, planning to find Persephone and bring her home. But Hades caught them and imprisoned them in chains that made them forget who they were and why they were there.

Demeter's grief was such that she prevented the earth from yielding its bounty. Winter came, the ground became cold and hard and nothing would grow. The mortals she had loved and cared for, and who looked to her for nourishment, starved and froze until in desperation they pleaded with Zeus to intervene. The god, realising that soon there would be no-one to make sacrifices to him, commanded Demeter to appear before him. She refused. Zeus admitted defeat, and sent Hermes to the underworld to fetch Persephone and return her to her mother.

When Hermes found her, she was seated beside Hades, sorrowing. She had refused all food and drink and was in a state of deep depression. Hades agreed to set her free, but only on condition that she would first eat some pomegranate seeds. Unaware that this would bind her to him forever, Persephone took and ate a few and Hermes escorted her back to Eleusis.

Demeter was so ecstatic at the sight of her daughter that the earth warmed and spring came. Plants, crops and flowers burst forth and the earth was bountiful once more. But when she discovered that Persephone had eaten the seeds of the pomegranate, she realised that her daughter was hers on loan only. If food or drink was taken in the underworld, a pact was made that ensured only a temporary stay away from that realm. The earth immediately grew cold once again.

Finally a compromise was reached. Persephone would spend a portion of each year with her mother and a portion with Hades in the underworld. The number of seeds that she had eaten were to mark the number of months that she must spend with Hades. Demeter had no choice but to reluctantly agree.

When Persephone made her annual journey to the underworld, Demeter marked her period of mourning by withdrawing her life-giving energy from the earth, and the seasons became marked by the relationship of mother and daughter. The springtime comes with Persephone's joyful return to her mother, the summer shows the warmth of their mutual love, the autumn marks the decline as they prepare to be parted, and winter comes when Persephone leaves Demeter to make her journey to the underworld.

Personality Traits

Demeter is the archetype of the devoted mother who does all that she can to protect her offspring from harm. This love is all-encompassing. The glow of her warmth spreads to touch all of humanity, who benefit from her generosity, just as a new mother holding her child experiences a rush of love and compassion that becomes universal rather than merely personal.

As earth goddess, Demeter was the embodiment of abundance. She taught mortals the arts of agriculture, and her benevolence and fertility were a source of boundless nourishment to all. The word 'cereal' stems from her name as the Roman Ceres, and the cornucopia is a symbol of the rich harvest of the gifts of the earth.

Her child was of primary importance to her. When Persephone was abducted, Demeter's grief was so overwhelming that the Earth itself became barren. The love that she bore for mortals was discounted under the weight of her despair at losing her daughter. She was the expression of maternal love and protectiveness at its most powerful, and her rage at Hades' abduction and Zeus' withdrawal from the situation made her immune to the pleas of the starving mortals, who had for so long been enfolded in her embrace, and of the gods who each brought gifts to her to attempt to persuade her to change her mind.

Yet even in her distraught state she was not fully closed to others. When she realised that Persephone was in the underworld, she disguised herself as an old woman and travelled to Eleusis. Queen Metanira, taken in by Demeter's appearance, took her on as nursemaid to her baby son, Demophoon.

The child grew strong through Demeter's nurturing and she determined to bestow on him the gift of immortality. Each night she placed him in the fire and each day she fed him ambrosia, the food of the gods. But one night Queen Metanira entered the chamber and, seeing Demeter apparently about to kill her son, was aghast. Demeter then revealed her true nature and demanded that a temple dedicated to her should be built. Eleusis later became the site where the Eleusinian Rites were held each year, re-enacting the story of Demeter and Persephone.

Demeter's willingness to give immortality to a mortal child illustrates how the mothering instinct cannot be quashed, even in times of great stress and grief. Her desire to protect her daughter extended to the human child who was in her care.

Relationships

Demeter's first relationship was with her parents. Unlike her brothers, who claimed their kingdoms and immediately left to go and rule them, Demeter was close to her mother, Rhea, and carried on the heritage of earth goddess that had passed through the female line from Gaia, to Rhea, to Demeter. All of these goddesses had great pain inflicted on them by their consorts and rebelled against them in order to protect their children. Gaia plotted against Uranus. Rhea enlisted the advice of Gaia and Uranus to prevent Cronus from swallowing any more of his children, and Demeter's helplessness in the wake of Zeus' uncaring attitude towards Persephone led to the onset of winter on Earth. The relationships of these three goddesses with the father-figure were strained and marred by abuse and this in turn affected their choice of mate and led to their affections being transferred to their children.

The coupling of Zeus and Demeter occurred before Zeus married Hera. Because of this, she was not subjected to Hera's jealous fury, as were the many who came after her.

Demeter had no desire for other relationships after the birth of Persephone. Her daughter provided the receptacle for the full focus of Demeter's love. This was so intense that it spilled over to engulf the Earth itself and all living things.

Sibling Rivalry

The most noteworthy relationships between Demeter and her siblings were those with Zeus and Hades. Zeus was her first and only lover and the father of her daughter. Hades was the abductor and husband of Persephone. Until that event occurred, Demeter had maintained a cordial though somewhat detached relationship with Zeus. She loved her daughter so dearly that she viewed the past relationship as the means through which she had attained her heart's desire. As Hades was rarely seen beyond the underworld, it was only when he deprived Demeter of Persephone's presence that he re-entered her consciousness.

Her grief and rage towards both of her brothers was immense. She reacted by withdrawing into herself and closing down the life-supporting benevolence that had nurtured those on Earth. Even as king of the gods, Zeus could not persuade or force Demeter to make the earth fertile again.

Although she was eventually reconciled with her daughter, she had to agree to share her with Hades. The seeds that Persephone had eaten had bound her to her husband and his realm. Demeter showed her mettle by refusing to give up the fight for her daughter, but had no choice but to honour the agreement. Yet she still was powerful enough to state her own terms. While Persephone was absent each year, winter would hold the Earth in its cold embrace.

Archetypal Resonance

Demeter as an archetype embodies all-encompassing mother love, the deep inner drive to give birth and to nurture and protect from harm. The element within the psyche that yearns to look after others is expressed through the maternal instincts that seek any available avenue of expression. This can manifest as a literal, physical experience of motherhood, or in the 'motherly' type of person to whom others turn for support and some tender loving care. An aspect that marks out the Demeter archetype is reflected when the needs of the children or friends take precedence over the needs and wishes of the husband or partner, which can engender resentment. The benevolent side of Demeter is prominent in all those who radiate acceptance and unconditional love. Whether or not they are literal or symbolic mothers, there is a fecund quality that has the effect of encouraging growth and the development of self-esteem in those around them.

The powerful elements in the story of Demeter and Persephone illustrate different aspects of this archetype. Firstly, she is the devoted mother who keeps her child close to her and who inspires total love and trust in return. But this protectiveness can be stifling if overdone. One of the tasks of motherhood is to encourage the child to learn independence and autonomy in a safe space. Each step towards this gradually opens up new vistas, until eventually the child is grown and has the self-confidence to take her place in the adult world. Demeter's devotion to Persephone was such that the child remained a child, even when she came of marriageable age. She was so strongly attached to her mother that their relationship was symbiotic and all others were viewed as insignificant or unnecessary. This ultimately is not a healthy situation, and what transpired with Hades created a sudden wrench for both mother and daughter that forced Persephone to enter the adult world, and Demeter to eventually accept that her daughter was now a woman as well as her child.

On the day that Persephone was abducted she had strayed out of her mother's sight and was gathering flowers in a meadow. Her innocence and ignorance of the world beyond the tightly knit relationship with Demeter was total. Hades emerging from the earth to carry her off signifies the shock that accompanies the end of childhood if no preparation has been made. Persephone, because of her closeness to Demeter, was unprepared, and the separation took her into a state of depression that accentuated her passivity. We cannot live out our adult lives under the protective umbrellas of our mothers, even should we wish to, because the urge towards growth and autonomy is instinctual. Persephone had strayed momentarily beyond Demeter's influence and this provided the opportunity for Hades to rush in and capture her. Demeter's control over Persephone (albeit willing on both sides) was substituted by that of Hades.

Another element in the story of Demeter and Persephone is the anguish of the mother who has lost a child. The process of mourning cuts off all access to the flow of the life-force, as when Demeter brought winter to the land. Only when a focus emerges for the nurturing energy, as with Demeter and the baby Demophoon, can healing begin. Those with a strong Demeter connection can experience a similar sense of loss of purpose and depression when the children grow up and leave home.

The shadow aspect of the archetype comes to the fore when the flow of mutual love is blocked. Demeter withdrew her fertile nature from the Earth, and the mortals and animals that she had sheltered and loved were placed in the precarious position of struggling to survive. When the darker elements of the goddess come to the fore, the Demeter archetype can be experienced as a withdrawal of love, nurturing and support; the destructive 'dark mother' who is too locked into her own feelings to be aware of those of others.

The fullest expression of the Demeter archetype lies in the will and the ability to love deeply, to protect, to nurture and to foster a sense of self. The greatest challenge comes through learning to let go; through accepting the knowledge that love includes the need to allow our loved ones the freedom to live independent lives. When this occurs, the sense of security that is an innate aspect of this bond ensures that they will always return, but as mature adults rather than as eternal children.

In Your Natal Chart

The position of the asteroid Ceres in the natal chart reveals how we experience and work with issues of nurturing and being nurtured. The relationship with the mother can be more clearly defined and understood and also our own attitudes towards parenting. The astrological sign that Ceres is found in acts as a lens for our perception of needs. This shows whether we feel loved or cherished and whether the bond with the mother has been loving, suffocating, or ambiguous.

Our attitudes towards our children (whether these are of the body or the mind) are reflected in the astrological sign that Ceres rests in. Whether we will be nurturing, detached or possessive is indicated. Attitudes around childcare and relationships are also signified by Ceres' position, along with issues of sexuality. If Ceres is prominent in the natal chart, the male in a woman's life can feel insignificant compared with the children. If the voice of Ceres is balanced by other archetypal voices such as Venus/Aphrodite or Juno/Hera, then the relationships with children and partner are likely to be more balanced and constructive. The nurturing power of Ceres can then be channelled into the creation of a nucleus of love and warmth that has a vitalising effect on all others who enter its sphere.

Ceres in the houses reflects how we go about ensuring that our emotional and physical needs are nurtured. Our willingness and ability to seek out the experiences that we need in order to foster a sense of self-love, and the areas of experience that will provide the outlet for this, are shown through the house position.

Aspects to Ceres indicate whether our ability to nurture and our acceptance of nurturing from others is free-flowing or blocked. Challenging aspects have the effect of either generating over-possessiveness, which has an inhibiting effect on our loved ones, or, conversely, an inability to relate to and connect deeply with those around us. Positive aspects to Ceres reveal healthy, wholesome family relationships that generate a strong sense of self-worth and trust. These create feelings of abundance, and family life is viewed as fertile ground that encourages growth, while also providing security.

Rulership of Ceres

The primary rulership of Ceres is in Cancer, with the strong maternal instinct of that sign connecting profoundly with the Ceres/Demeter archetype. Cancer's planetary ruler, the Moon, denotes the tides of life, the ebb and flow of fertility through the menstrual cycle, and the attitudes towards mothering and nurturing. The area of the body ruled by Cancer is the breasts, the source of nourishment for infants. Ceres' rulership of this sign travels deeper into the blood and milk areas of maternity, whereas Artemis, as cool Moon goddess, manifests less as the physical mother and more as the protector of women in childbirth.

In Cancer, Ceres' qualities of deep attachment and uncondi-tional love, and her role as the matrix of security, are evident. Also prominent is the typically Cancerian retreat into a hard shell when hurt. Demeter's refusal to listen to others while she was grieving over the loss of Persephone, and her chosen isolation from the world she loved and which depended on her, is markedly similar to the Cancerian reaction to pain. The Cancerian gift of enveloping loved ones in a rosy cocoon of caring and sharing is also attributable to Ceres – not only with Persephone, but also with the mortals to whom she gave the fertile abundance of the earth.

There are indisputable connections between the possessiveness of Cancerians and Ceres. Relationships, whether romantic or familial, are so vital to the Cancerian psyche that well-being is strongly bound up with the physical closeness of the loved one. The leash is often short and tightly held, as Cancerians tend to want their beloved to remain in the immediate vicinity. The mother who needs to know where her child is at every moment, even when that child has grown; the child who clings closely to the apron-strings of the mother; the partner who needs the constant physical presence of their significant other – this is the type of love that Demeter and Persephone shared. Often the break, when it comes (as it must, in order for the child to grow up) is sudden and traumatic.

Cancerians have a reputation for being good cooks. Food is important to them for physical nourishment, but is also viewed as a means of giving and demonstrating love. By feeding others they can express their innate nurturing capabilities, both physically and emotionally. Ceres' role as earth goddess, her gift of agriculture to mortals, and her qualities of nourishing and nurturing accord closely with the Cancerian nature.

Ceres is also connected to Virgo. The image of the goddess holding a sheaf of grain is very similar to the pictorial representation of Virgo. Virgoans are less noted astrologically for their maternal instincts (though many Virgoans do carry the role of earth mother well) because of their conventional reputation for purity and chastity. Yet the qualities inherent in nurturing others are pronounced in this sign. The Virgoan attention to the well-being of those around them, the focus on nourishment through careful attention to the food that is prepared, and the element of service to others all resonate with the Ceres archetype. Yet in the case of Virgo the focus on food is for the maintenance of health, rather than as an emotional issue.

Virgoans need to feel that they can contribute in some way for the good of humanity. This bears a resemblance to Ceres' love of mortals. She chose to live among them, she taught them agriculture and she was prepared to gift the baby Demophoon with immortality − to raise him to her level spiritually. The Virgoan nature strives to help others, with no expectation of reward and, as an Earth sign, Virgo has a strong connection with the processes of life and growth.

However, the Demeter–Persephone connection, with its co-dependency and inability to let go on both sides, is more apparent in the sign of Cancer. Although Ceres holds a resonance that sings through both Cancer and Virgo, it is in the sign of motherhood that her voice is heard most powerfully.

CHAPTER FOURTEEN

Juno ⚵
Hera

Hera is the embodiment of commitment. Despite the trials inflicted on her by Zeus, her husband, she holds firm and refuses to give up on their marriage. Her pride distances her from the other Olympians, and her fury brings disaster to the lives of those who refuse to honour the sanctity of marriage.

Her integrity in holding to her principles is unshakeable within a family that views casual liaisons as the highly desirable norm. Her willingness to repeatedly take her husband back is mirrored among the immortals only in the marriage of her rejected son, Hephaestus, to Aphrodite. Hera holds to her beliefs despite formidable opposition because her sense of identity is closely bound up with the position she holds.

The Birth of Hera

Hera, like the other children of Cronus and Rhea, was swallowed by her father at birth. When she emerged from the belly of Cronus, she lived with Oceanus and Tethys, Titan children of Gaia and Uranus, until Zeus, allied with the Titans, had overthrown his father. When

Zeus took the throne and set the scene for the Olympian era to begin, Hera left her foster-carers and went to live in Olympus.

Her beauty was enchanting, but she was chaste and refused to give herself to any man before marriage. After Zeus had indulged in affairs with others, including his sister Demeter, who bore him Persephone, his roving eye alighted on Hera and he pursued her. Hera, however, rebuffed him until he turned himself into a cuckoo during a storm and nestled at her breast. Hera's sympathies were aroused and when Zeus returned to his immortal form she agreed to be his consort on condition that he married her.

Initially the marriage was happy, but then Zeus resumed his philandering and Hera, as goddess of marriage, was mortified and furious. She took revenge on the lovers of Zeus rather than on her husband, which still did not deter goddesses, nymphs and mortals from responding to his advances.

Hera bore associations with the pagan Great Goddess, the triple goddess of life and death. In ancient tales the milk that flowed from her breasts created the Milky Way. This connection filtered into the mythology of the Olympians, and Hera was considered to be the queen of Heaven and the equal to Zeus.

Personality Traits

There are two distinct aspects to Hera's personality. Homer took a very negative view of her and portrayed her as the vengeful, vindictive, henpecking wife who sniped at her husband and punished his paramours harshly. This judgement has tended to override Hera's positive qualities and to give her an unbalanced and unpleasant reputation.

She did wreak terrible vengeance on those who coupled with her husband. Leto, the mother of Artemis and Apollo, was forced to wander the Earth in search of a place where she could give birth because none dared risk Hera's wrath through coming to Leto's aid.

When Zeus seduced Callisto, who was a member of Artemis' band of forest nymphs, he disguised himself as Artemis in order to get close to her, and she bore him a son, Arcas. Later, when Hera found out, she changed Callisto into a bear and tried to trick Arcas into unknowingly slaying his mother. Before he could do so, Zeus intervened and transformed him into a bear too, then placed mother and son in the heavens as Ursa Major and Ursa Minor, the bear constellation.

This vindictive side of Hera stemmed from her view of marriage as sacred. Her sense of self was inextricably tied in with her role as wife and consort. To leave Zeus permanently was unthinkable to her, although on several occasions she fled from Olympus and retreated within herself until the emotional wounds had begun to heal. Then she would return, there would be another brief honeymoon period and Zeus would resume his philandering. And so the cycle continued.

His affairs and his large brood of illegitimate children caused Hera great anguish. That Zeus could sully their relationship was hurtful and humiliating for her, yet she could not bring herself to make him suffer for his behaviour. His children by other women were less fortunate.

Dionysus, the god of wine and ecstasy, was the son of Zeus and Semele, a Theban princess. The Romans called him Bacchus and the rites carried out in his name were wild and orgiastic. His followers, the maenads, would enter into frenzied, ecstatic states that often culminated in debauchery and dismemberment. Hera tried several times to kill him and succeeded in driving his foster-parents insane, but Dionysus proved too strong for her. Eventually he died at the hands of his maenads and his grave was placed at Delphi. For the months of the year while Apollo retreated to Hyperborea, Dionysus took charge of the Delphic oracle.

Of the Greek heroes, the strongest was Heracles, the son of Zeus and Alcmene, and known to the Romans as Hercules. His mother had married King Amphitryon of Tiryns, on condition that the consummation of the marriage would take place after Amphitryon had taken revenge on the murderers of her brothers. While the king was away carrying out his task, Zeus came to Alcmene disguised as her husband and told her that the deed had been accomplished. She went into his arms willingly and Heracles was conceived. When her husband returned, he found that Alcmene was under the illusion that he had already taken her virginity and eventually the truth became known.

Heracles' name meant 'Hera's Glory'. Zeus appears to have assumed that Hera would be flattered. Instead she was deeply insulted and outraged, and made every attempt within her power to destroy Heracles, ignoring Zeus' explanations as to why he had deliberately created this child. He knew that there would be a battle between the gods and a race of giants, and intended that this son would be a mortal of such strength that his opponents would be defeated. Hera hated Heracles. She sent two snakes to kill the baby, but the infant slew them. Later she caused him to go insane and murder his wife and three children. His remorse at what he had done led him to undertake the Twelve Labours of Heracles, accomplishing feats that were considered to be beyond the power of any mortal. It was also Heracles who negotiated with Zeus for Chiron to take the place of Prometheus in Tartarus and be allowed to die and be reborn yet again as an immortal.

As a mother, Hera had none of the nurturing qualities of her sister Demeter. When Zeus birthed Athena parthenogenically from his forehead, Hera retaliated by conceiving Hephaestus without the help of her husband. The child was born with a club foot and Hera, furious that he was not perfect, hurled him from Olympus to Earth. In another version of the story, Hephaestus remained with Hera until he took his mother's side in an argument with Zeus, and it was Zeus who threw him from the heights of Olympus. Hephaestus later married Aphrodite, who was the only other goddess to enter wedlock, and he was subjected to a similar marital situation to Hera, with his wife flaunting her unfaithfulness.

Ares was the son of Zeus and Hera and also disappointed his parents. He had none of the cool logic that was respected by the gods, and both parents disliked him intensely because they considered him to be impetuous, foolhardy and bloodthirsty, and were blind to his more appealing qualities. Their daughters, Hebe and Eileithyia, remained in the background of the Olympian pantheon.

But despite her indisputably dark side, Hera was worshipped by the Greeks (and later, as Juno, by the Romans) as the benevolent goddess of marriage, whose blessing could bestow sanctity and happiness on the marital state. Rituals were held in her honour and, in keeping with her association with the pre-Olympian Great Goddess, the triple goddess in her aspects as maiden, mother and crone, three separate rituals were dedicated to her each year.

The celebration of the maiden aspect of this was held in the springtime, the mother aspect in the summer, and the crone aspect in the winter. These seasons of a woman's life were portrayed symbolically. Spring saw Hera as the virginal maiden, summer was the consummation of her marriage, and winter marked her season as the wise old crone, the widow who holds a direct connection with death.

The Sacred Marriage

The sacred marriage that Hera represented was more than merely the physical union between man and woman, god and goddess in the eyes of the world. Hera's perception of marriage was the purity and sanctity of the coming together of the highest, most spiritual aspects of male and female; a combination that led to mystical experience. All levels of being were integrated in this — physical, emotional, mental and spiritual. This sacred marriage embodied a true merging of souls and a uniting of opposites. The search for a soul mate, the elusive 'One' is the contemporary vision of access to the most potent domain of Hera.

This was Hera's vision of the marital state. Before wedding Zeus she had high ideals about the joys and responsibilities involved. To then discover that her husband held an entirely different view, and considered all females as commodities and receptacles for his seed, was a profoundly devastating experience for his idealistic wife. Her response was violent and extreme, but perhaps unsurprising.

Relationships

Hera had no relationships before marrying Zeus. Like Persephone, she was an innocent maiden, but whereas Persephone had no desire to leave her mother, Hera felt that marriage was the highest state that could be attained. She was not an earth mother like Rhea and, like all of the first-generation Olympians, had to contend with an infanticidal father. As daughter to a nourishing mother and a father who was overthrown by his son, she followed the pattern of entering into an abusive relationship.

Zeus loved her, but felt no desire or need to be faithful to her, despite her obvious rage and anguish each time she discovered the presence of another paramour. She left him several times and wandered the Earth, hiding the shame she felt when faced with the sly glances of the other Olympians. But each time she returned, because she could not imagine her place as being anywhere but at her husband's side. She was the epitome of faithfulness, loyalty and devotion where Zeus was concerned.

Siblings

Hera was sensitive to her situation as first lady of Heaven and consort to Zeus, and his casual attitude towards her was a source of public humiliation for her. By virtue of her marriage she was set apart, and her vengeance on those who lay with her husband was so terrifying that the other goddesses avoided her.

She was not close to her siblings and had no confidantes. She had a competitive streak and her beauty was a source of pride to her. The Trojan War was sparked by a contest between Hera, Aphrodite and Athena over who was the loveliest. They chose Paris, son of the king of Troy, to award a golden apple to the most beautiful of the three goddesses, and each tried to bribe him in order to gain his favour. Hera offered Paris rulership over the lands of Asia, Athena offered him victory in war, and Aphrodite offered him the love of the most beautiful woman in the world. Paris awarded Aphrodite the golden apple, but the woman in question was Helen, who was married to King Menelaus of Greece. The war that ensued between Greece and Troy after Paris and Helen eloped ended after ten years with the defeat of Troy.

Archetypal Resonance

Hera as an archetype embodies the qualities of loyalty and commitment in a relationship. This is experienced psychologically as the urge towards union with another. But whereas with Aphrodite it is the spark of attraction that provides the impulse towards romance and sensuality, for Hera this union comes about through a deep need to have a 'significant other' in her life. Casual relationships are not for her. Instead, this archetype manifests as the desire to be with one special person who will honour her in an enduring relationship. The young girl who is eager to have an engagement ring on her finger that she can show off to her friends, the young woman who rushes into marriage with high ideals and expectations of a permanent happy ending are both typical expressions of the Hera archetype.

If this is not forthcoming and there is no significant relationship, the feelings of isolation and purposeless can be intense and painful. Until recently a woman defined herself, and was defined by others, through her husband. Feminism changed attitudes and enabled women to assert that they could be happy and fulfilled whether single or married. But the Hera archetype still holds her place in the psyche, and if her voice is strong then the urge towards a committed relationship is the overruling consideration.

This can be seen in abusive relationships, where the woman is urged by others to leave for her own protection and safety, or that of her children, but cannot bring herself to take that step out of the marital sphere. Like Hera, she cannot consider the abandonment of the husband as a prospect.

In a healthy relationship based on trust and respect, the Hera archetype thrives, and the bonds that are forged between the partners serve as an inspiration to all who know them. Together they appear to add up to more than the sum of each individual, and the relationship itself takes on what amounts to a separate identity to those within it. It casts a radiance that shines through each of them. Hera can now fulfil her role as goddess of the sacred marriage and bestow her highest blessings.

However, if the partner is unfaithful when the Hera archetype prevails, retribution is swift and sometimes deadly. The crime of passion, which in some countries is still seen as a justifiable act more than as a punishable offence, is a result of the dark aspect of Hera. Her persecution of the lovers of Zeus and their children was an extreme reaction that is often reflected in less dramatic ways in contemporary society.

The need to love and be loved is the primary concern of the Hera archetype and is exacerbated by the need to be seen to be cherished by a mate and to feel a certain status as a result of this. But the voice of Hera needs to be heard alongside other voices if she is to be happy. The independence of Athena or Artemis can enable her to invest less of her sense of self in the person she is with. For Hera cannot feel complete without a mate who is willing to be a life-partner.

Her family is secondary to her husband and the Hera archetype may even resent the attention that her children demand from her, or be jealous of the love they receive from her spouse if, like Athena, they stand high in their father's favour.

A predominant Hera tends to choose a strong mate, an alpha male. She needs to feel secure, protected and proud of him. When Zeus came to Hera as a small, helpless bird, soaked from the rainstorm, he aroused her sympathy. But it was when he revealed himself as the most dominant god that she was willing to give herself to him, providing that he sealed their union formally.

The fullest expression of the Hera archetype lies in her ability to be loyal, to stand beside her partner no matter what happens. Her devotion is absolute and her love is unwavering. Hera's capacity for commitment is such that she deserves the respect and consideration that she yearns for.

In Your Natal Chart

The position of Juno in the natal chart reveals our attitudes towards, and experiences of, committed relationships. When Juno is a strong influence in the chart, there is a desire, and even a powerful need, to seek out a serious long-term partner. The astrological sign that Juno is placed in is an indicator of the type of partner that you will be attracted to and also shows your mode of expression within that partnership. The house that Juno rests in denotes how that need for union will be channelled.

If Juno's voice is quiet among the archetypes in the natal chart, it is more likely that this urge towards relationship will be channelled into other areas of life. Juno is a forceful character and is not generally attracted to people who are less powerful than herself. When there is no driving urge towards marital relationships, Juno's considerable energy can be directed instead towards business partnerships or friendships. The sexual aspect of union is less important to her than the feeling of trust and belonging.

When there are positive aspects, the Juno energy is experienced as tremendous loyalty, dedication and devotion. Relationships are likely to be enduring because Juno ensures that the needs of both partners are met and because compromise is possible during rough patches. Negative aspects to Juno can manifest as possessiveness and jealousy — even friends can be viewed as a threat — and a strong competitive urge that has no compunction about knocking the competitor out of the picture. Slights are taken to heart and there can be problems over issues of trust.

Juno in the natal chart also gives clues about the attainment of a sense of fulfilment and the ability to express the nobler aspects of the female nature. There is a strong idealism present in this archetype and this can be a force for the good when properly channelled.

Rulership of Juno

Juno is most aptly suited to the rulership of Libra, the sign of partnership. The Libran urge to connect with another at a deep level is directed through Juno at a specific relationship that is carefully nurtured and fostered.

Of the astrological signs it is Libra who often finds it most difficult to be alone. Librans need others for friendship and companionship, and the sense of isolation that can result if this is not forthcoming can make them depressed or physically ill. The creativity and love of beauty that are characteristic of Libra are both attributes of Juno. Her beauty, and the need for others to 'see' that and appreciate it, reveals that she has more in common with Aphrodite/Venus than initially meets the eye. But although Aphrodite can be flighty, and even promiscuous, and is driven by the desire to merge fully with another in order to experience the alchemy of union, her attention tends to stray once the first flush of romance has faded. Juno, however, brings a constancy and a desire for the security of an enduring relationship.

One of the symbols for Juno is peacock feathers. Their iridescent colours and the eye in the centre symbolise the goddess's pride and watchfulness. Little escapes her notice, and she rages against what she views as injustices. In Hera's story it is the willingness of other women to be seduced by her husband and therefore betray their sisterhood that renders her incandescent with fury, to the extent of attempting to destroy those who sully the sanctity of marriage. Although the usually gentle Libran is less likely to wreak havoc, if they are faced with situations of injustice, their sweet exterior will quickly disappear and they will not hesitate to gird themselves and take action. 'It's not fair' is a rallying call to Librans and they are prepared to pour all of their energies into a cause that they consider to be worthy.

Juno and Librans prefer an ordered environment where the gaze can rest on beauty and harmony. This is important to their well-being and they are disturbed by disorder, both internally and externally, because it interferes with the sense of peace that they crave. This is also true of their appearance. Beautiful clothes, jewellery and fragrances strengthen their sense of self, because both Juno and Librans need to feel accepted and admired by others.

Equality is a major issue: in the relationship with a loved one, in friendships and in the workplace. If Juno or Libra feel unappreciated, then sparks can fly and, if the situation remains unchanged, they will retreat until a solution or compromise can be found. When their needs for equal consideration are met, harmony reigns and they are able to express their inner strength, poise and charm.

The darker element of Juno also relates to the astrological sign Scorpio. The intensity of Hera/Juno leads to extreme vengefulness as retaliation to acts of betrayal. To Scorpios a loss of trust is initially devastating, then transforms into a cold fury that is capable of destroying everything in its path. Possessiveness is an aspect of the Scorpio nature, especially in relationships. The loved one must be theirs alone and this can create power struggles and control issues. In the story of Zeus and Hera, Zeus was well aware of the effect that his infidelity had on his wife. Yet he was prepared to cause her agonising emotional pain and put the lives of his lovers and their children at risk in order to prove to her that he could do as he pleased.

Because the marriage was stormy after the long honeymoon period came to an end, there were frequent battles for control between Zeus and Hera. As leader of the gods, Zeus considered that he deserved every privilege available. Hera was his equal, but Zeus was very much the alpha male. As the humiliated wife, Hera made bids to control him through harming the recipients of his sexual favours. The Scorpionic refusal to give in, the impulse to battle to the death if necessary, is strongly emphasised when there are strained aspects to Juno.

Yet even the darker elements of Scorpio have the ability to achieve their redemption because of Juno's rulership. The attributes of willpower, tenacity, loyalty, and lasting attachment that cannot accept defeat are also borne out by Juno's affiliation with this astrological sign.

CHAPTER FIFTEEN

Pallas Athene ♀

Athena

Although a virgin goddess like Artemis and Hestia, Athena's temperament is very different to the wild Artemis and the gentle, spiritual Hestia. She swore early on to give her body to no man, and her sharp intellect and skill in battle make her equal to both male gods and mortal men. Born motherless, she is powerful and independent, not given to displays of emotion, and commands loyalty and respect.

Athena's focus is on honing the mind and body to create a unified tool for clarity and effectiveness. Strong, wise, an adept strategist, she makes decisions based upon careful consideration, and refuses to act on impulse. Her self-sufficiency makes her formidable to those who are less capable. Her joy is in the perfect harmony of body and mind as an instrument of the will.

The Birth of Athena

The parents of Athena were Zeus and the Titaness Metis, the daughter of Oceanus. Metis was renowned for her wisdom and herb lore and it was she who, after the defeat of Cronus, prepared the emetic herbs that forced Cronus to regurgitate the children he had swallowed at birth in order to try to prevent his own overthrow.

When Metis conceived, Zeus was warned by Gaia and Cronus that she would give birth to two children. The second, a boy, would take the throne of Zeus and rule in his stead. To avoid this, Zeus tricked Metis into becoming small and then swallowed her. He avoided the birth of a son by Metis that was predicted by his parents, but Athena grew within his forehead until the pain was so great that Zeus commanded Hephaestus to relieve the pressure by splitting open his forehead with his axe. Athena sprang out wearing golden armour and a helmet and carrying a spear. She became the favourite daughter of Zeus, displaying the qualities of wisdom and intelligence, logic and a cool head in battle that her father greatly admired.

Personality Traits

Athena was very much a man's woman; a trait that was highly unusual and earned her great respect among the male Olympians. She was beautiful and proud, courageous and level-headed, and became an asset to Zeus, and the only person whom he consulted about strategies. She was a mentor to many of the heroes and acted as protector and advisor to them.

Perseus was one who benefited from her support. When she discovered that Poseidon had seduced Medusa in one of her sacred places and had turned the beautiful Medusa into a fearsome gorgon with snakes for hair, she decided that Medusa must be slain. She advised Perseus to use his shield as a mirror so that he would not have to look upon her face, for to see the visage of Medusa would turn men to stone. When he confronted the gorgon, Athena guided his hand so that the sword he was wielding cut cleanly and Medusa was killed. She then took the head and mounted it upon her shield. Pegasus, the winged horse who sprang from Medusa's neck, was tamed with a golden bridle that Athena gave to Bellerophon for that purpose.

When Heracles was driven insane by Hera and killed his wife and children, Athena aided him in carrying out the twelve labours that he had to undertake in order to attain redemption.

The Trojan War, which lasted ten years and caused the death of many heroes, began when Paris, the son of King Priam of Troy, abducted the beautiful Helen, whom Aphrodite had rewarded him with as the prize for choosing her as the loveliest of the goddesses. Athena, through her anger at Paris, sided with the Greeks and came to their aid repeatedly. Her favoured hero was Achilles, the son of King Peleus of Thessaly and the sea nymph Thetis.

Poseidon and Zeus both desired Thetis and wished to have a child by her. But they were deterred from pursuing her when Prometheus warned them that her future son would be more powerful than his father. Instead, Zeus arranged for her to be married to a mortal and, soon after, Achilles was born. Thetis dipped her child in the waters of the River Styx, which flowed through the underworld, in order to make him immortal. She held her son by his heel, which then became the only part of his body to be left unprotected.

Achilles learned the art of war from Chiron, who was his tutor and mentor. He was ferocious in battle, but even Athena could not save him when Paris discovered his vulnerable spot and shot an arrow into his heel, killing him.

Athena's sympathies were always with the men. When Orestes, the son of the hero Agamemnon and his wife Clytemnestra, killed his mother, Athena spoke up for him and insisted that he be set free, arguing that Orestes had been justified in committing matricide. While Agamemnon had been away fighting in the Trojan War, Clytemnestra had taken a lover. When her husband returned ten years later, she and her lover murdered him. In despair and fury Orestes slew his mother – the worst crime that could be committed in Ancient Greece. It was only through the intervention of Athena that his life was spared.

Athena was proud of her 'male' attributes. She felt no hesitation about plunging into battle, and her admiration and friendship were reserved for men who were strong and courageous warriors and heroes. As daughter of the goddess of wisdom and the king of the gods, she inherited the most potent qualities of both parents and despised those who were emotional or foolhardy.

As a virgin goddess she was insistent that no man could touch her. Her physical energy was channelled into warfare and her mental energy into the pursuit of knowledge. When Hephaestus attempted to rape her, Athena pushed him away. His semen fell to the ground and fertilised the earth. Gaia used her generative powers to birth a snake, Erichthonius, the serpent of wisdom, which Athena took to live with the oracle and interpret the prophecies. A statue of Athena with a snake was later placed in the Acropolis in Athens, symbolising the attributes of wisdom and the power over life and death that she held.

Her rulership of Athens came about when the inhabitants of the city decided to choose a guardian deity. Both Athena and Poseidon put themselves forward and each bestowed a gift to the citizens in order to influence the choice. Athena gave an olive tree and Poseidon a small spring. The Athenians chose Athena, and Poseidon vented his anger by flooding the plain that surrounded the city. The city was named after Athena, and the olive tree became one of her emblems.

The totem creature of Athena was the owl. Its reputation for wisdom and knowledge, its ability to see in the dark and strike instantly when prey appeared, and its silence in flight, were qualities that Athena identified with.

Her competitive nature was aroused several times: once when Paris declared Aphrodite to be more beautiful than Athena, once when she and Poseidon vied for rulership of Athens and again when her ambition to always be first and best among women was challenged by a mortal.

Athena and Arachne

One of Athena's domains was that of craftwork, because of the skills that are needed in the creation of artefacts of beauty and intricacy. Her skill in weaving was one that Athena was proud of. Her logical mind and her ability to see the completed article in her mind's eye, and to hold that image until it was transferred through her nimble fingers, made her a master weaver.

There are two versions to the story of Athena and Arachne. In one, Arachne's fame as a gifted weaver grew until other mortals were comparing her skill to that of Athena. In her fury, Athena turned her into a spider and the word 'arachnid' stemmed from her name.

In the second story, Arachne went to Athena and challenged her to a weaving competition. They each created a tapestry of great beauty, and Athena was impressed until she realised that the subject of Arachne's tapestry was Zeus in several of his guises in the act of seducing his paramours. Athena, closer to her father than to any other, was offended, insulted and enraged. She destroyed the tapestry, and Arachne hanged herself. But before the mortal woman could die, Athena changed her into a spider that hung by a silken thread and devoted its life to spinning webs of great beauty and intricacy.

Relationships

Athena was a virgin goddess in the fullest expression of the term. She was self-contained, needing no other in order to be fulfilled and experience a sense of completeness within herself, and chaste. Unlike many of the other goddesses, who were at the mercy of their emotions, Athena was detached and cool, ruled by her head instead of her heart.

She preferred the company of men, where she could be accepted and respected for her understanding of warfare and for her keen intelligence, and she was close to Zeus. Her sensual energies were diverted into intellectual and creative pursuits and she had no desire for a consort. Her pleasure was gained through being viewed and treated as an equal. Because of this she was the least vulnerable of the goddesses. When she was slighted, her retaliation was swift and merciless, but when her support was aroused she was always willing to do all that she could to help those whom she favoured.

Athena's clear head made her a good strategist and she was instrumental in giving advice and guidance to many of the heroes, who revered her and were intensely loyal to her.

Born from her father's forehead, active in the world of male gods and mortals, Athena appeared to have no thoughts of her mother, whom Zeus had imprisoned within him. She was disinterested in the traditional womanly pursuits, wiles or grievances that she observed around her and was determined to remain true to herself.

Siblings

Athena took a detached attitude towards her family, other than her father. Hera was deeply jealous of Athena's relationship with Zeus, particularly as Zeus had birthed Athena parthenogenically. Her ill-fated retaliation in birthing Hephaestus led to her rejection of him because he, with his club foot, could not compete with the beautiful and powerful warrior goddess. Later, Athena's half-brother Hephaestus' attempt to rape her was rebuffed but the snake that issued from his seed as it fell to ground strongly embodied her symbolic aspects, and she adopted it as her child. Athena's distrust in emotional matters meant that when it was strategic for her and her 'step-mother', Hera, to join forces temporarily against Zeus, it was accomplished without any unnecessary hard feelings on either side.

Her relationship with Ares was strained. He was envious of her position as joint favourite (with Apollo) of his father, and Athena scorned his hot temper and inability to stay calm in battle. She also despised him for taking the side of the Trojans in the war and enlisted Zeus' permission to fight against him, ensuring that he was wounded.

Archetypal Resonance

Athena as an archetype embodies the qualities of intelligence, creative thinking, strategy-making and emotional detachment. Her position as a woman among men, in which she displayed the attributes of logical thinking, forward planning and the courage and determination to fight for her convictions, makes her a powerful archetypal force.

Within the psyche she is the voice of reason: strong, ambitious, undeterred by others' opinions of her unless she considers them to be worthy of respect. She is the epitome of cool, clear logic that is able to see straight to the crux of a matter and refuses to be distracted from the task at hand.

This archetype steers clear of messy emotions that interfere with the powers of reasoning. If relationships are entered into, they are viewed more as a form of contract in which each person has an agreement, rather than through a rosy vision of romantic love that is considered to be both distasteful and foolish. If the contract is broken, the relationship is terminated.

Sexual impulses are often sublimated and diverted into channels that create mental rather than physical involvement, though it can also be viewed as a useful commodity. A love of knowledge opens the doors to serious academic study. An attunement to beauty and symmetry makes creative outlets that require planning and skill very appealing.

The Athena archetype is a gifted negotiator, mediator and diplomat through her clear-sightedness and ability to examine a situation so that the most logical, workable course of action is clear. She earns respect from others, although she can be emotionally distant. Athena's golden armour represents the tendency of this archetype to guard against showing any form of weakness, as this is anathema to her. There is a need to be viewed as strong and self-sufficient, with no chinks visible that could make her vulnerable. This armour protects her on two levels: on the first it gives her privacy and security; on the second it allows her to avoid intimacy and to keep a sense of autonomy. The gold of her armour also reflects the radiance of her mental faculties and insights.

The need to maintain independence and to be valued for her intellectual and perceptual gifts is the driving motivation of Athena. A respect for these qualities in those around her is her point of connection with others.

In Your Natal Chart

The name 'Pallas Athene' stems from pre-Olympian times, when the triple goddess who contained within her the combination of maiden, mother and crone was known in Libya as Pallas, Athene and Medusa. Pallas was the virginal maiden, pure and clear-sighted. Athene was the mother of creative intelligence that manifested as fecundity, and Medusa was the crone in her guise as the death-dealing devourer of men. These three aspects became merged in Ancient Greece, and Athena incorporated these as the wise and intelligent virgin goddess who was a fearsome opponent. She was also known to the Romans as Minerva.

In the natal chart, Pallas Athene's position reveals how we use our intelligence and powers of logical thinking. A hunger for knowledge, clear perception and talents in devising and following through plans and strategies are the qualities that Pallas Athene brings to the horoscope. When this archetype is strong and positively aspected, there is tremendous insight, perception, planning power, strength, courage and independence. A need for physical as well as mental activity is prevalent and this can result in a love of sports, particularly where these involve competition against others. Mental interests encompass a wide range to include any facility that provides knowledge and adds to understanding.

Strategic games such as chess are also popular with the Pallas Athene archetype.

Negative aspects to this asteroid can manifest as frustrating mental blocks, a conviction that others must always be in the wrong, and a refusal to listen to reason. The independence of Pallas Athene, when badly aspected, can lead to a harsh determination to win at any cost and illustrates the saying that 'the end justifies the means'. Conversely, some negative aspects can drain the self-confidence that provides the foundation for independence and can contribute towards a secretive, introverted personality who is more interested in books or their computer than in people.

Athena's role as protector of and mentor to heroes is reflected in the natal chart as a strong sense of justice that, as with Hera / Juno, is very much on the side of who or what is 'right'. If justice is not done, then this archetype will go into battle with her armour shining and her weapons aimed with unerring accuracy. The force of will is such that the battles fought are rarely lost, because Pallas Athene is able to plan out the most effective tactics in advance.

The astrological sign that Pallas Athene is found in denotes the manner through which Athena's influence is felt in the natal chart and in the psyche. In Taurus, for instance, her creative and intellectual faculties are channelled into creating works of beauty that appeal to the senses yet also have intellectual or symbolic meaning. In Libra, she can manifest as a mediator and diplomat who is skilled at negotiating and sprinkles her elegant speech with words and phrases that are calculated to make an impact without causing offence.

Pallas Athene in the houses shows the areas of life in which intellect, independence, self-confidence and determination will be channelled.

Rulership of Pallas Athene

Pallas Athene is most at home in Scorpio, the sign of indomitable will. The penetrating Scorpio mind is able to work well with Pallas Athene's gift of perceptiveness and ability to formulate strategies that take all sides of a situation into account. Scorpios tend to be excellent strategists because they are able to hide their thoughts from others while being aware of undercurrents, and they can plot an accurate course to their goal by observing which influences are around, and then make allowances for these. Like Pallas Athene, Scorpios dislike the thought of making mistakes, and take care to ensure that they have everything under control.

The art of war, which Athena is skilled in, is the domain of Scorpio. Mars will rush in recklessly, following his impulses and becoming caught up in the heat of battle to the extent of losing his head. Scorpio, like Pallas Athene, has the inner drive and the passion for winning, but is able to be patient, to plot the course that will be most effective and that will ultimately lead more swiftly and surely to victory. Like Athena, Scorpios refuse to show signs of weakness. Their armour is strong and, once a course is set, nothing can deter them from following it through. Respect for others whose strength is equal to theirs is predominant, as is a willingness to advise and protect those who are prepared to put effort into helping themselves. As enemies they are merciless and will stop at nothing. Athena's determination to have Medusa slain by Perseus for sullying her sacred space is a heightened demonstration of the lengths to which the Scorpionic nature can be prepared to go in order to exact revenge.

Although Scorpio is considered to be the most sexual of the astrological signs, this energy can also be symbolised by the kundalini, an element in the subtle energy system of the body. Scorpio rules the base chakra, the area where the kundalini is seated. The symbol for this is two snakes that entwine up the spine as they awaken and uncoil and this represents the transformation of sexual energy into spiritual illumination. The Scorpio ability to utilise this as a means of channelling the physical urges into a clear perception of a mentally and spiritually awakened state resonates strongly with Pallas Athene's totem of the snake.

CHAPTER SIXTEEN

Vesta

Hestia

Hestia is an embodiment of the virgin goddess, along with Artemis and Athena. Hers is the realm of spirit; not the numinous, intangible realm of Poseidon, but the glow of the inner flame that lies at the centre of the self and lights the way homeward.

The most retiring of the Olympians, Hestia prefers to exist in all homes and hearts rather than reside only with the gods, far from the reach of mortals. The flame that represents her is the flame of life itself that can be transferred from heart to heart and hearth to hearth. Hestia embodies the sanctuary, both within the self and in the home and temple, where the self finds physical and spiritual sustenance.

The Birth of Hestia

Hestia was the oldest of the Olympian siblings. Born first and swallowed by her father, Cronus, she was the last to leave his body when he regurgitated his children. Of all her family she was the only one to retreat from Olympus voluntarily, choosing instead to exist in a spiritual rather than humanised physical form. She was greatly revered and worshipped as the guardian of the hearth and also as the keeper of the sacred flame of life.

The quietest and most retiring of the Olympians, Hestia remained in the background, beyond the confines of the rowdy family circle yet present as a unifying force. The symbolism of her Sacred Flame endures to the present time: the Olympic Torch is lit from Hestia's flame, and marks the beginning of the Olympic Games – a celebration of the strength and endurance of the body and the power of the spirit that fuels the physical form.

The Hearth

The goddess elected to be portrayed as a flame rather than as a physical form. Her nature was the homeland of warmth, inspiration, nourishment and comfort, and the circular hearths and temples that were built in her honour represented the unbroken circle of life and the wholeness encompassed within it. Hestia chose to live within the home and heart of every deity and immortal.

The hearth was the central focus of the home, where families could gather together and be warmed by its fire and by the company of each other. As the fire was also used for cooking food, it was the source of nourishment as well as heat. Gazing into the flames could elicit visions and meditative states and open the mind to the silent spaces within, where spiritual insights could be accessed. As goddess of the hearth, Hestia's flame burned within every home, creating a connection between each member of the family with the wider community. The first flame in a newly built hearth was ceremonially carried there from its source, the mother-fire, so that the essence of the goddess spread to encompass all.

In each home was an altar to Hestia and she received the choicest offerings of all the deities, yet offended none of her siblings, who also revered her. Her physical and spiritual presence, felt through the warmth of the fire, was a constant reminder of her guardianship.

The Temple

In pre-Olympian times the goddess principle was worshipped in an earthier manner than during and after the rise of the Olympians. The followers of the Great Goddess, in her triple aspect of maiden, mother and crone, were guided by priestesses who tended the sacred flame of life. Although considered to be virgins in the sense of being independent and autonomous, they were also sexually active in the service of the Great Goddess. The men who came to learn more about the nature of the goddess were taught by these followers to respect the sexual and spiritual union of the god and goddess within. Children born from these rites were considered to be a gift from the goddess.

With the coming of the Olympians, Hestia embodied the connection with the soul, with the eternal flame that burns within. The sacred marriage of the union of god and goddess aspects took place within the self, integrating the anima and animus within the psyche and opening the perception to a knowledge of the spiritual realms through devotional practices and a simplicity of lifestyle.

Hestia and her Roman counterpart, Vesta, vowed to remain virgins and refused all offers of marriage. The Romans built a circular temple to Vesta where her maidens, the vestal virgins, lived and worshipped. These were chosen at a young age, usually at around six years old, and were contracted to remain at the temple in the service of Vesta for thirty years. After that time they could leave, though most of them chose to stay. The rules were strict. The sacred flame must be continually tended and never allowed to go out; chastity, purity, devotion and humility were essential. If these rules were broken, the punishment was harsh. A vestal virgin who lost her virginity was condemned to a slow death, buried alive under the ground. Vesta's maidens held privileges not bestowed on other women. They were autonomous, independent from men, free of the patriarchal rules of society, and revered beyond the confines of the temple. The vestal virgins were given charge of contracts and important documents, as their purity and respect for the privacy of others made them supremely trustworthy.

Personality Traits

Hestia was gentle and quiet. She chose not to live on Olympus; instead, the hearth and fire were living embodiments of her. As a virgin goddess she was self-contained, complete and had no need of any outer trappings to cultivate her sense of self. Whereas the other virgin goddesses, Artemis and Athena, chose companions (for Artemis it was her nymphs, for Athena her heroes and warriors), Hestia preferred solitude. Although her vestal virgins lived in the temple dedicated to her and kept her eternal flame alive, Hestia's presence was felt by all people, everywhere, through the hearth fire. She asked for no offerings or special treatment other than that her fire was kept burning, yet was the best-loved of the goddesses. Her calm poise and her connection with the spiritual nature shared by all were traits that others sought and strove to emulate. Her focus was on the total absorption with the spiritual self that made any task, however mundane or dreary, an act of devotion and dedication.

Her detachment held nothing of the coolness of Athena. It was a detachment fostered by the understanding that the dramas and longings of life were essentially born from a yearning for unity with a force greater than the small, limited self. Because of this, every action took on an aspect of sacredness that created a sense of harmony and connection with the life-force. Her loving nature was apparent each time a fire warmed the surrounding air.

Hestia was set apart from the relationships between the other gods and goddesses. She had no interest in petty jealousies or conquests. Instead she preferred solitude, with its wide-open spaces within the mind, where thoughts could soar to touch the Infinite. Unlike her siblings, she was unconcerned about external appearances or others' opinions of her. Her sense of peace and completeness set her apart and allowed her to observe all from a state of tolerant compassion.

Relationships

Hestia rejected all advances that were made to her. Her sexual impulses were channelled into her inner self, and the purity and calmness that she radiated gave her an aura of quiet confidence. The active nature of Artemis and Athena found expression in hunting and warfare. In Hestia this was directed into meditation and contemplation.

Poseidon and Apollo, her brother and nephew, both wished to marry her, but Hestia declined their offers and gently asserted her wish to remain chaste and pure. She was no doubt an attractive prospective wife for both of these powerful gods; the embodiment of the still, calm centre for the stormy-natured sea god, and a haven of peace and tranquillity for the god of the Sun, whose yearly retreat to Hyperborea was needed to recharge his energy. Instead, Zeus agreed to allow Hestia to remain virginal and made her the gift of a place within the hearth of every home.

Siblings

Although Hestia was insular, she was closely associated with Hermes through their guardianship of the home. Whereas Hestia's sacred place was the hearth and fire, Hermes was the protector of the threshold, the border between outside and inside. These two deities ensured that the home was a place of safety and security. The old marriage custom in which the husband carries his wife over the threshold of a new home is in honour of Hermes. An altar would be set up by the hearth, where both deities could be honoured.

Archetypal Resonance

Hestia as an archetype embodies the search for meaning and the fostering of simplicity in life. She is the quiet, calm voice in the psyche that needs to be carefully listened to in order to be heard among the more assertive voices of the other archetypes. A need for time alone, an urge towards a spiritual approach to life, and a love of silence and perception of holiness (inner wholeness) in every task that is carried out are all attributes of Hestia.

This self-contained goddess steps to the fore whenever there is the wish to allow the world to drift by while you sit and watch in peace, uninvolved in the noise and drama. Fastidiousness is one of her aspects, because the body and mind are equally respected, and the body is understood to be the temple of the soul. And 'soul' is a word that resonates closely with Hestia, in the sense of the life within. The soul of a painting, of music, of dance, of the minutiae of daily tasks carries the demonstration of the life-force that fuelled the activity. This is experienced as a continual expression of the light of the inner world as it radiates through to the outer world.

In Your Natal Chart

Vesta's position in the natal chart reveals how and where you seek out inner stillness and silence. The brightest of the asteroids, it shines its light through the sign and house that it is found in, gently encouraging us to express a commitment to a lightness of being that is detached from worldly cares and considerations. The sacred fire that Vesta embodies is the flame of inner warmth and nurturing accompanied by a strong yet peaceful sense of self. This flame, when combined with aspects to other planets, can be fanned by the breath of sensuality and sexuality that views sex as a sacred act of pure love and devotion. The ancient role of Hestia / Vesta as an embodiment of the Great Goddess still lives within us and can be awoken if the right person appears; one who has an attitude of relationship as the joining of the inner as well as outer male and female.

Without aspects between planets that can act as the prince to the Sleeping Beauty of Vesta's purity, the asteroid brings a focus to the sign and house that it is found in which allows independent thought and action, compassion without attachment, and profound thought and insight.

If there are challenging aspects to Vesta, this can manifest as either a fear of solitude because we are reluctant to delve too deeply into the meanings and purpose of challenges in our lives, or, conversely, there can be an aloofness that creates a personality that is cut off from others and from the life-force. Issues around sexuality are prominent in difficult aspects to Hestia, which can take the form of frigidity, promiscuity or confused relationships, because the sense of self is weakened, and therefore vulnerable or undefined. The boundaries that Vesta maintains can be either ineffective, or built so high that they imprison the self, depending on which aspects are involved.

When strong and well-aspected in the natal chart, Vesta helps to define a clear-cut sense of self and purpose and a keen, enquiring mind that seeks to illuminate itself. There is a propensity for hard work because work is viewed as service. The ability to connect with the sacred and the spiritual in all aspects of life and a warm, calm demeanour are expressions of Vesta. Love is easily inspired because there is a soft glow that emanates from the core of being and elicits a welcoming warmth from others in return.

Rulership of Vesta

Vesta is the ruler of both Virgo and Scorpio, and the connection with Virgo is immediately apparent. The pictorial symbol for this sign is the virgin carrying a sheaf of grain, denoting connections within the Virgoan nature with both Vesta and Ceres/Demeter. In its rulership of Virgo, Vesta accentuates the qualities of purity, chasteness, clarity of thought, dedication, devotion to others through service, and detached aloofness. The calm Virgoan exterior hides an active inner life and through Vesta the realms of the spirit are accessed.

Unless strongly aspected, the Virgoan attitude towards relationships has a noticeable affinity with Vesta. Virgoans are more content to be alone and single than any other sign in the zodiac. Their independence and autonomy is highly valued. Their love of cleanliness and order makes them good housekeepers and homemakers, but the main motivation for the maintenance of tidiness, harmony and cleanliness is that an uncluttered environment helps the mind to be clearer.

Virgo's perfectionism is reflected in Vesta's insistence upon truth and order and a clear code for living that is based upon honesty and integrity.

The connection with the sacred space of the home is held by Mercury and Vesta. As the pillar that guards the threshold of a dwelling, Mercury provides a source of male strength and independence. As the circular hearth within, Vesta provides the female source of warmth and light. Part of Virgo's self-sufficiency is the inner recognition of both the god and goddess within.

Vesta's rulership of Scorpio is less immediately apparent until we remember the pre-Olympic role of this luminous goddess. The rites to the Great Goddess were performed between the priestesses and the men who came to them to honour the goddess in both her physical and spiritual form. The sexual acts that took place were transcendental, transforming the climax of each participant into a spiritual charge that elevated them to the temporary status of god and goddess. The union was viewed as complete within itself and relationships were not forged between the priestess and the men other than during the single experience of the act of transformation. Children born from this were considered sacred. The sexual act was, in essence, a contract between man and priestess to strive for the highest spiritual state: a circumstance that exists to the present day in the practice of tantra, the art of ecstasy that leads to enlightenment.

In Vesta's rulership of Scorpio, this is the attitude towards physical pleasures. Because of Vesta's high ideals and extreme choosiness, coupled with a strong sense of self that makes it difficult to surrender fully to another person, the combination of this sign and asteroid leads to discrimination when selecting a partner. Vesta is a perfectionist, and in its own way, so is Scorpio.

The Scorpionic intensity of thought and need to discover causes and hidden meanings is made profound by Vesta's rulership. Scorpio's urge towards transformation and renewal is symbolised by the inner flame that Vesta embodies. Just as the phoenix, a Scorpionic totem, hurls itself into the fire only to be reborn, so does the Scorpio nature eagerly enter the flames of transformation in order to die as the old, limited self and re-emerge more potent and powerful from the renewal of the connection with the sacred.

CHAPTER SEVENTEEN

Relationships and Aspects

An understanding of the relationships between the deities whose myths underpin the symbolism of the planets can make the interpretation of the astrological aspects much easier and clearer.

The aspects are the mathematical relationships between the planets that demonstrate an effect on the mode of expression of each planet involved. Some aspects are beneficial, others create tension, but all of them create a point of connection that is vital to an understanding of the dynamics of the natal chart. The following are examples of how you can interpret the aspects through their archetypal resonance as well as in the traditional manner.

An easy way to work out the dynamics of the deities through the aspects is to imagine that you are having a party and that each archetype is one of your guests. If Venus and Mars are in conjunction (very close to each other), the sexual sparks that fly between them could add an interesting charge to the atmosphere, because Aphrodite and Ares were lovers. Conversations between other guests might be less noticeable than the dialogue that is taking place between these two. Their energy could bring added vitality and spark to the party, or could leave some guests feeling rather embarrassed if the aspects to them are more chaste. Pallas Athene might find the situation irritating and irrelevant, and try to bring some culture to the floor show. Vesta might quietly withdraw, unless other connections are present through the aspects that bring Hestia's earthier, pre-Olympian role to the fore.

Now, as all of the guests are elements of yourself, the dynamics are taking place within your psyche, and the choices as to whether you choose to ignore what's going on between Venus and Mars, or enjoy it, or interrupt with an intellectual conversation is entirely up to you. The connections between the archetypes are revealed through your natal chart, but the channels that are present for the expression of these in your life can be understood and worked with so that it is ultimately more beneficial for you.

The Conjunction ☌

A conjunction occurs when two planets sit side by side in the natal chart. Its orb (sphere of influence) is between 0 and 8 degrees. Often a conjunction is positive, but its effect can be detrimental, depending upon the planets involved, as this aspect brings added strength to both of the planets that are in relationship.

Example

A conjunction between the Sun and the Moon, for example, brings together the twin children of Zeus and Leto, Apollo and Artemis. This can create tension, as their individual modes of expression are very different.

The willpower and competitive nature of these siblings can cause a clash similar to that which occurred when Apollo duped Artemis into killing Orion, her lover. The forcefulness of the Sun is then rejected by the retiring nature of the Moon, and strength is temporarily lost. This is most powerful when aspects are also made to other planets in the natal chart. If Mars is connected to either planet, the active aggressive principle will be activated, which will bring dominance to that planet. So if Mars is linked to the Moon, Artemis will subvert the willpower of Apollo. If Mars is linked to the Sun, the emotions and intuition will be ignored and the logical mind will be dominant.

When the Sun is conjunct with Mercury in the natal chart, the two brothers Apollo and Hermes stand side by side. They need a certain distance in their relationship, as it began on the wrong footing in the Greek myths, with Hermes stealing Apollo's prized cattle. However, their differences were resolved after Hermes gave his lyre to Apollo, and a truce was called.

The astrological interpretation of a conjunction between the Sun and Mercury depends on how close the planets are to each other. If they are 'joined at the hip', with an orb of less than 4 degrees, this creates what is called a 'combust' conjunction. Both planets, literally, are combustible; they burn each other out. You can imagine this as a fight between the two brothers from which both emerge bruised and exhausted, with no power left for anything else. The astrological effect is that of an overabundance of solar energy that literally 'fries the brain' and makes the thought processes confused. Neither side wins. If there is a safer distance between Apollo and Hermes, they can get along very well. The creativity and urge to self-expression of the Sun can spark off the intellectual capabilities and communication skills of Mercury. This brings positiveness and eloquence to the personality and makes you popular.

The Sextile ✶

A distance of 60 degrees between planets, with a 5-degree orb either side, is called a sextile. This is a harmonious aspect that brings about friendly relationships.

Example

A sextile between Venus and Saturn brings interesting possibilities. Cronus, Saturn's deity, symbolises the need to work with limitations and impose discipline. In the myths, he swallowed his children in order to hold on to his power, then was taken up by the Romans and became their fatherly, fertile god of agriculture. Venus is free-flowing, a creative and social butterfly. They would not make an obvious good match.

Venus embodies beauty and harmony and artistic gifts. Saturn embodies restraint and boundaries. A sextile between these two planets is often found in the natal charts of talented artists, because Saturn gives the self-discipline that enables beautiful ideas to take form. The gift of creativity needs this in order to bring shape to ideas.

The Square □

When there is a distance of 90 degrees between two planets (with an orb of 8 degrees) this is called a square and is an indication of challenges that need to be dealt with. These can either overwhelm you or be used as a springboard to achievement. Often it is the challenges that we face that test our mettle; our determination to overcome these can bring added strength to the personality.

Example

In the Greek myths, the relationship between Zeus and Ares was very strained, and this is exacerbated if there is a square between Jupiter and Mars, their astrological counterparts. Zeus despised Ares because of his inability and refusal to employ logic. The rashness and impetuousness of his son's nature irritated him in the extreme. In turn, this rejection by his father only served to make Ares more rebellious and determined to go his own way. Their relationship was one of intense dislike and conflict.

A square aspect between Jupiter and Mars echoes this situation within the psyche. The Jovian expansiveness and power is diverted into aggression and a destructive attitude that leads to extremes of behaviour. Jupiter's benevolence becomes twisted into a desire for self-aggrandisement, and the approach to others can be harsh and dictatorial.

However, a positive aspect such as a sextile can ease the strain between the two archetypes. The energy and drive of Mars can instead be utilised by Jupiter's optimism and urge towards growth and expansion. The difficult relationship between father and son can be healed as each discovers that the other has qualities that are valuable and constructive.

The Trine △

When there is a distance of 120 degrees between two planets, with an 8-degree orb, this is called a trine: a beneficial aspect that brings out the very best in the archetypes who are linked by it.

Example

A trine between Jupiter and Uranus brings together the highest qualities of both deities and planets. In the myths, Uranus was the grandfather of Zeus. His reign was terminated when his son Cronus emasculated him, and he retreated into the background. But as the first sky god, whose generative power was contained within the forces of thunder and lightning, he bequeathed his thunderbolt to Zeus, who only used it as a weapon when absolutely necessary. The beneficial interaction between their planets brings the powers of thunder and lightning to the fore in the form of sparks and flashes of creative insight and inspiration. The expansive nature of Jupiter is then able to increase the electro-magnetic properties of Uranus and this manifests as true leadership qualities and the ability to perceive solutions to problems that are not apparent to those around them. The combined energy of these two powerful sky gods brings a depth and profundity of thought, and even flashes of genius.

The Opposition ☍

An opposition is found in the natal chart when two planets are placed directly opposite each other, 180 degrees apart, with an orb of 8 degrees. Oppositions create tension, rather like two people facing each other in an argument, though occasionally the old saying that 'opposites attract' can be true in astrology as well. Dialogue or intervention is necessary in order for balance to be achieved, and other aspects to one or both of the planets concerned, such as sextiles or trines, can help to defuse the potential for internal psychological conflict.

Example

If Ceres and Pluto are in opposition in the natal chart, this can bring about an internal scenario that is similar to the mythological situation between Demeter and Hades. In the story, Hades abducted Persephone, the beloved daughter of Demeter, and carried her off to the underworld to be his wife. Demeter's grief was such that she shut down the fertility of the earth until her daughter was returned to her. Yet even after Persephone's return it was necessary for her to share her time between Hades and Demeter, because she had undertaken a contract to him before she left.

An opposition between Ceres and Pluto indicates that there will be power struggles in life based on attempting to hold on too tightly to that which is dear to you. The fear of loss is so great that the creative urges can be used destructively, and the challenge set by the opposition is that of learning to let go and compromise.

Soul Patterns

If you hold the stories of the myths in your mind, this can be very useful in understanding the dynamics that are prevalent between the planets involved. Each planet represents an element within the psyche, and the archetypal patterns that emerge from their relationships can enable you to discover resolutions to difficulties that allow new strength and growth. But the aspects have more to tell you.

When the natal chart is set up and lines are drawn between the planets that are mathematically connected, a pattern can be seen. This picture is a mirror of the soul and enables you to have an image of what motivates you to discover and carry out your purpose in life.

The natal chart is a map of the heavens at the moment of your birth, as you would see it if you could look up at the sky as a newborn child. The birth chart is the key to your personality and potential and can be used to unlock the secrets of the inner self. The aspect pattern can help you with this. The shapes that are made can be read intuitively. You may see the combination of lines as a flower, or a butterfly, or pyramid or boat. Allow your imagination to fly free when you look at the aspect pattern and it will reveal much of your soul life. The spark of recognition that this can engender can have a transformative effect on how you view yourself.

Astrology is a complex science, and there are many good books that can enable you to interpret your natal chart step by step through the planets in the signs and houses, and through the aspects. The skill then is to develop the ability to integrate the information. As the purpose of this book is the connection between the myths and the planets, an in-depth interpretation of all of the factors that can be taken into account in the natal chart is not included. But the stories of the deities can open up a fresh perspective on the journey of discovery that fuels the study of astrology. The ancient myths that still live on within the psyche enable us, through their resonances with the planets, to better understand ourselves and others.

CHAPTER EIGHTEEN

Harmonising the Voices

Everything in the universe – the 'one song' – is vibration, and each vibration carries a sound, however subtle. We may not hear it but we can feel it deep within us. Sound carries great power. It can heal, uplift, energise, relax and destroy. Our moods and mental states are affected by the sounds around us; the music we listen to can prepare us for meditation or for sleep, for housework or for partying. Being woken by birdsong puts us in a very different frame of mind to being woken by road drills outside our window.

The symphony of the universe, the humming of the spheres as they travel unimaginable distances across space, comes together as countless musical notes whose range is far greater than the diatonic scale that we use on Earth. And something deep within us responds to it, because we are part of it. The range of the mind is limitless; it can travel on a beam of light, can create new worlds in an instant. In quantum physics it has been discovered that the act of observation creates the form, in a wave or particle, that the observer expects to see – and that form then endures forever. The power of our mind and our imagining is infinite.

Within the mind is the potential for all that we could become and also within it is the negator of that potential, the swallower of the creative children of our imagination. The choices that we make about whether or not to allow ourselves to fulfil our potential are based on whether we pay attention to the voices of the inner self that whisper in our psyche. The archetypes, singing through the clashing or harmonising chords in the mind, are brought to light and to life through their planetary counterparts in our natal chart. Some make their voices heard more than others but they are all present, offering their gifts and their challenges, arguing among themselves, making love, making war, creating harmony or discord. If we accept them and honour them, we learn to accept and honour ourselves. If we work with them, they can lend us the strength and power to fulfil our purpose. But first we need to reach for the volume controls.

When the noisier archetypes are allowed to have their own way, it can be at the expense of the quieter ones. If you are in a room where one or two people are shouting above the music, the music itself appears to become discordant. When this happens in the natal chart, we can turn down the volume, adjust the bass and treble and find more inner balance and harmony. The loudest voices may not be the archetypes that you would expect from the myths; it may not be Mars, or Mercury or Jupiter. It could be Pluto, who keeps you in the underworld, cautioning you to wear your cap of invisibility like Hades. It could be Vesta, telling you that relationships are not necessary, or Ceres, saying that all that matters is the role as parent. What is important is to find balance and use your gifts wisely and well.

The natal chart reveals our strengths and weaknesses. We can utilise our understanding of the archetypes to turn down the volume of the ones who are taking control and find ways to allow them to be better integrated with the others. And we can play up the strengths and learn to develop them. If the planetary configuration has elements of inner conflict that hold you back, you can reduce this by observing the harmonising elements and obtaining their help. If Mars and Jupiter are squaring up (literally preparing for psychological conflict), you can enlist the help of Venus, with her loving nature, or of Pallas Athene, with her logic and skills in mediation. Vesta may be called upon to allow a quiet inner space where resolution can be found, or Mercury, who can encourage inner dialogue between the warring elements and act as the guide through to the light of joy and release. We are never entitled to use our natal chart as an excuse for not resolving inner challenges. Obstacles are present so that we can learn to negotiate them and grow stronger through that process.

Often the quietest voices in the psyche are the ones that can offer the most wisdom, and the loudest voices are those that clamour for our attention in order that we may allow them the harmony they crave. By looking at who is seated where in the mind's pantheon, and listening to what they have to say, we can find ways that allow them to be heard more clearly and open ourselves up to increased inner harmony and unity.

Archetypal Rulerships

Aphrodite / Venus rules Venus, Taurus, Libra and the 2nd and 7th Houses

Apollo rules the Sun, Leo and the 5th House

Ares / Mars rules Mars, Aries, Scorpio and the 1st and 8th Houses

Artemis rules the Moon, Cancer and the 4th House

Athena / Pallas Athene rules Pallas Athene, Scorpio and the 8th House

Chiron rules Chiron, Virgo, Sagittarius and the 6th and 9th Houses

Cronus / Saturn rules Saturn, Capricorn and the 10th House

Demeter / Ceres rules Ceres, Cancer, Virgo and the 4th and 6th Houses

Hades / Pluto rules Pluto, Scorpio and the 8th House

Hera / Juno rules Juno, Libra, Scorpio and the 7th and 8th Houses

Hermes / Mercury rules Mercury, Gemini, Virgo and the 3rd and 6th Houses

Hestia / Vesta rules Vesta, Virgo, Scorpio and the 6th and 8th Houses

Poseidon / Neptune rules Neptune, Pisces and the 12th House

Uranus rules Uranus, Aquarius and the 11th House

Zeus / Jupiter rules Jupiter, Sagittarius, Pisces and the 9th and 12th Houses

Index

Achilles 126, 160
Actaeon 37
Adonis 56–7, 66
Aethiopians 23, 103
Agamemnon 160
Alcippe 66
Alcmene 148
Amphitrite 104–5
Amphitryon 149
Aphrodite 22, 47, 66
  archetypal resonance 58
  birth 53–4
  essential qualities 53
  personality traits 54–5
  relationships 56–7
  sibling rivalry 57
  the Transformer 56
  see also Venus
Apollo 45, 73, 128–9
  archetypal resonance 32
  birth 25–6
  essential qualities 25
  jealousy of Orion 31, 38, 43
  personality traits 26–7
  prophecy 27–8
  relationships 29–31
  sibling rivalry 31, 35
  see also Sun
Aquarius 76, 99–100
Arachne 161
Arcas 148
archetypes
  harmonising the voices 185–7
  interpreting the forces 12
  and myths 12–13
Ares
  and Aphrodite 57
  archetypal resonance 67–8
  birth 63–4
  essential qualities 63
  personality traits 64–5
  relationships 66
  sibling rivalry 67
  warrior and dancer 65–6
  see also Mars
Ariadne *see* Theseus
Aries 70–1
Aristaeus 30

Artemis (Diana)
  archetypal resonance 39
  birth of 25–6, 37
  essential qualities 36
  and Orion 38, 43
  the Protectress 37–8
  relationships 38
  see also Moon
Ascalaphus 64
Asclepius 30, 126
aspects *see* relationships and aspects
asteroids 15–17, 123–4
astrology 20, 98, 124
Atalanta 54–5
Athena (Minerva) 152
  and Arachne 161
  archetypal resonance 164–5
  birth 158–9
  essential qualities 158
  personality traits 159
  relationships 162–3
  siblings 163–4
  see also Pallas Athene
Atlas 31, 45
Autolycus 47

Bacchus *see* Dionysus
Bellerophon 159

Cadmus 66
Calliope 30
Callisto 148
Cancer 42–3, 143–4
Capricorn 90–1
Cassandra 29
Castor and Pollux 103
Cerberus 30, 113
Ceres
  discovery 123
  natal chart 142–3
  rulership 143–5
  see also Demeter
Chaos 14–15, 21, 93
Chiron
  archetypal resonance 129–30
  birth 126
  discovery 123
  essential qualities 125

natal chart 131–2
personality traits 126–7
relationships 128–9
rulership 132–3
siblings 129
wounded healer 127–8
Clytemnestra 160
conjunction 179–80
Coronis 30
Cronus 22
archetypal resonance 87
birth 82–3
God of Time 84
personality traits 83–4
relationships 85–6
Saturnalia 84–5
sibling rivalry 86
see also Saturn
Cyclopes 94
Cyrene 30

Danae 77, 105
Daphne 29
Deimos and Phobos (Fear and Panic) 57, 64, 65, 66
satellites of Mars 69
Delphi 22, 27
Delphinus 104
Demeter 22, 75, 86
archetypal resonance 140–2
birth 134–5
essential qualities 134
and Persephone 105–6, 135–7
personality traits 137–8
relationships 138–9
sibling rivalry 139–40
see also Ceres
Demophoon 138
Diana see Artemis
Dione 53
Dionysus (Bacchus) 28, 73–4, 148

eclipses 40
Egg of Night 21
Eileithyia 150
Eleusinian Rites 135, 138
Elysian Plain 23
Elysium 114
Erichthonius 161
Erinyes see Furies
Eros 21, 29, 56, 57, 66
Eudorus 47
Euridyce 30–1

Europa 77
Eurynome 75

Fates 24
Fear and Panic see Deimos and Phobos
Furies (Erinyes) 22, 24, 94

Gaia 21–2, 28
Ganymede 76, 99
Gemini 50–1, 103
genealogy of the early Olympians 23
Graces 24
Great Goddess 171

Hades 22
abduction of Persephone 114, 135–7
archetypal resonance 115–16
birth 111–12
essential qualities 111
personality traits 112–13
the Realm of the Dead 113–14
relationships 114–15
sibling rivalry 115
see also Pluto
Harmonia 57, 66
Hebe 150
Hecatoncheires 94
Helen of Troy 152, 160
Hephaestus 56–7, 149–50
Hera 22
archetypal resonance 152–4
birth 146–7
essential qualities 146
personality traits 147–50
relationships 151
sacred marriage 150–1
siblings 151–2
see also Juno
Heracles (Hercules) 112, 127, 130, 148–9, 160
Hermaphroditus 47, 52
Hermes 51–2, 73, 173
archetypal resonance 48–9
birth 45
essential qualities 44
the Messenger 46, 48
personality traits 45–6
relationships 47
sibling rivalry 47–8
see also Mercury
Herschel see Uranus
Hestia 22
archetypal resonance 173–4
birth 169–70

essential qualities 169
the hearth 170
relationships 173
siblings 173
the temple 170
see also Vesta
Hippolyta 55
Hippolytus 55
Hyperborea 23
Hyperion 22

Iapetus 22, 128

Jason 126
Juno
discovery 123
natal chart 154–5
rulership 155–7
see also Hera
Jupiter 85
natal chart 78–9
rulership 79–81
topography 77–8
see also Zeus

Leda 77
Leo 34–5
Leto 25–6, 37, 75, 147
Leuce 114
Libra 61–2, 155–6, 166

Maia 31, 45
Mars
natal chart 69–70
rulership 70–1
topography 68–9
see also Ares
Medusa 105, 159
Melanion 54–5
Memory *see* Mnemosyne
Mercury 176
natal chart 49–50
rulership 50–1
topography 49
see also Hermes
Metanira 138
Metis 73, 75, 158
Minerva *see* Athena
Minos, Rhadamanthus and Aeacus 113
Minotaur *see* Theseus
Minthe 114
Mnemosyne (Memory) 22, 75, 86

Moon
creation and topography 39–40
natal chart 40–2
rulership 42–3
see also Artemis
Muses 24, 75, 86
Myrtilus 47
mythological family 17–18
myths
and archetypes 12–13
cultural significance 14
early 21–2
and planets 15–16
and science 14–15

natal chart 184
Neptune
natal chart 108–9
rulership 109–10
topology 107–8
see also Poseidon
Niobe 37
nymphs 37–8

Oceanus 22, 146, 158
Olympian genealogy 23
opposition 183
Orestes 160
Orion 31, 38, 43
Orpheus and Euridyce 30

Pallas Athene
discovery 123
natal chart 165–6
rulership 167–8
see also Athena
Pan 47
Paris 152
Pasiphae 102
Pegasus 105, 159
Persephone 114
and Demeter 105–6, 135–7
Perseus 77, 105, 159
Phaedra 55
Philyra 126
Phoebe 22
Pirithous 136
Pisces 60, 80–1, 109–10
Plain of Asphodel 114
planets
creation 19–20
names 16–17

and mythology 15–16
planetary associations 15
Pleiades constellation 26
Pluto 116
    natal chart 117–19
    rulership 119–21
    topography 117
    see also Hades
Poseidon 22, 55, 115
    archetypal resonance 106–7
    birth 101–2
    essential qualities 101
    personality traits 102–3
    relationships 104–5
    Ruler of the Deep 104
    sibling rivalry 105–6
    see also Neptune
Priapus 64
Prometheus 128, 149, 160
Psyche and Eros 56
Pythia 28
Python 28
Pythonesses 28

relationships and aspects 178–9
    the conjunction 179–80
    opposition 183
    the sextile 180–1
    soul patterns 183–4
    the square 181–2
    the trine 182
Rhea 22, 72–3, 83, 138–9
Romulus and Remus 64
rulership 124, 188

Sacred Flame 170
Sagittarius 79–80, 132–3
Saturn 61
    natal chart 88–90
    rulership 90–1
    topography 88
    see also Cronus
Saturn's Return 89
science and myths 14–15
Scorpio 60, 71, 119–21, 124, 156–7, 167–8, 175, 176–7
Semele 74, 148
sextile 180–1
Sirius 31, 38
soul patterns 183–4
square 181–2
Sun
    creation and topography 32–3

in natal chart 33–4
rulership 34–5
see also Apollo

Tartarus 114, 128, 149
Taurus 60–1, 166
Tethys 22, 146
Themis 22, 25, 75, 86
Theseus 55, 102–3, 136
Theta 22
Thetis 160
Titans 22, 83–4, 94, 129
    see also individual names
Titys 37
trine 182
Trojan War 67, 75, 152, 160
Twelve Labours of Hercules 149, 160

Uranus 21–2
    archetypal resonance 96–7
    birth 92–3
    essential qualities 93
    natal chart 98–9
    personality traits 93–4
    relationships 95
    rulership 99–100
    siblings 95–6
    topography 97

Venus
    natal chart 59–60
    rulership 60–2
    topography 59
    see also Aphrodite
Vesta
    discovery 123
    natal chart 174–5
    rulership 175–7
    see also Hestia
vestal virgins 171–2
Virgo 50–1, 124, 132–3, 144–5, 175–6
voices, archetypal 185–7

Zeus 22
    archetypal resonance 76–7
    birth 72–3
    essential qualities 72
    personality traits 73–4
    relationships 75–6
    sibling rivalry 76
    Sky God 74–5
    see also Jupiter